HANDBOOK FOR RAILWAY STEAM LOCOMOTIVE ENGINEMEN

BRITISH TRANSPORT COMMISSION

Handbook for Railway Steam Locomotive Enginemen

IAN ALLAN Publishing

First published 1957
First reprint 1977
Second reprint 1998
Third reprint 1998
This impression 2000

ISBN 0 7110 0628 8

© British Railways Board 1957/1998

Published by Ian Allan Publishing

an imprint of Ian Allan Publishing Ltd, Terminal House,
Station Approach, Shepperton, Surrey TW17 8AS.

Printed by Ian Allan Printing Ltd, Riverdene Business Park,
Hersham, Surrey KT12 4RG.

Code: 0004/A

FOREWORD

The object of this book is to help enginemen to become proficient in their duties. In particular, it will be beneficial to cleaners and firemen in their preparation for promotion.

It is written with the object of giving a general description of locomotives and the principles involved in their construction and operation within the compass of a book of reasonable size.

The book deals with the steam locomotive, but it is the intention to follow it in due course with a similar publication dealing with other forms of motive power.

It should be emphasised that no one can become a proficient railway locomotive engineman merely by reading books, however good they may be. The highest proficiency, however, can only be achieved by studying the subject from all angles and putting into practice the knowledge and precepts gained from text-books.

The increased cost of fuel, together with the importance of punctuality, makes it essential that you should strive by all the means in your power to achieve the fullest knowledge of your work, and close study of this publication is one way which will assist you to do this.

R. F. HARVEY

Chief Operating and
Motive Power Officer

CONTENTS

SECTION 1

General *Page No.* 15
Introduction: Notices and Rules: Cleaners: Firemen:
Drivers: Working Trains: Engine Disposal: Turning the
Locomotive.

SECTION 2

Combustion *Page No.* 23
Composition of Air and Coal: What happens in the Firebox:
Principles of Good Firing: Preparing the Fire: Starting away
with the Train: Firing on the Journey: When the Regulator
is Closed: Blowbacks: Firing of Shunting Locomotives:
Size of Coal: Use of Fire-irons: Use of Deflector Plate: Use
of Dampers: Working of Injector.

SECTION 3

Transformation of Heat into Power *Page No.* 34
Heat: Temperature: British Thermal Unit: Conduction:
Convection and Radiation: Steam Generation: Relation of
Temperature to Pressure: Saturated Steam: Superheating.

SECTION 4

The Boiler: Boiler Mountings and Details *Page No.* 37
Types of Boilers and Fireboxes: Smokebox: Self-cleaning
Smokebox: Superheater: Blast Pipe: Brick arch: Firehole
Door: Drop Grates and Rocking Grates: Hopper Ashpans:
Boiler Mountings: Safety Valves: Water Gauges: Pressure
Gauges: Fusible Plugs: Washout Plugs: Handhole and
Mudhole Doors: Blower and Valve: Regulator Valve:
Vertical Side-type Regulator: Horizontal Dome-type Regu-
lator: Horizontal Regulator—Smokebox type: Double-beat
Regulator: Multiple Valve Regulator: Injectors: Exhaust

Injectors: Steam-controlled Exhaust Steam Valve: Auxiliary Shuttle Valve: Steam-controlled Water Valve: Possible causes of Injector Failures: Blowdown Valve: Carriage-warming Valve: Cab Fittings.

COLOUR IDENTIFICATION CHART

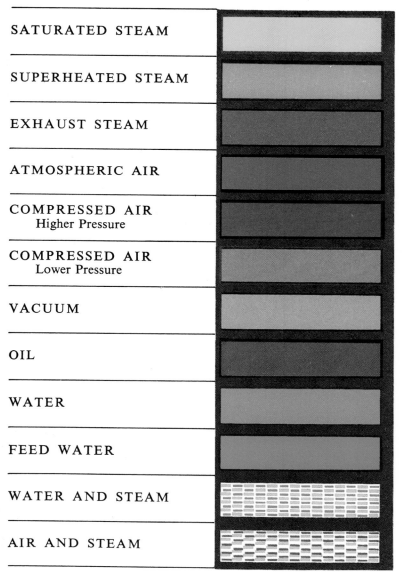

SATURATED STEAM	
SUPERHEATED STEAM	
EXHAUST STEAM	
ATMOSPHERIC AIR	
COMPRESSED AIR Higher Pressure	
COMPRESSED AIR Lower Pressure	
VACUUM	
OIL	
WATER	
FEED WATER	
WATER AND STEAM	
AIR AND STEAM	

The above colours apply to all diagrams except
where shown otherwise

DIAGRAMS

Fig. No. *Page No.*

SECTION 1

GENERAL

Introduction

The Junior Engine Cleaner who has started his career to become an Engineman on British Railways is expected to take an interest in locomotives, to fit himself to take charge of them when he is promoted. Whilst working as a Cleaner he must make himself acquainted with the general arrangement of the various types of locomotives and learn the names of the various locomotive parts, e.g. frames, cylinders, steam chests, wheel arrangements, boiler, firebox, smokebox, safety valves, etc. He will receive tuition from Chargeman Cleaners, Firing Instructors and Inspectors. He should take the opportunity to supplement the information in this Handbook by asking questions of Fitters, Drivers, Firemen, Foremen, Inspectors, and by attending Mutual Improvement Classes, and lectures in the Mobile Instruction Trains, where provided.

Notices and Rules

In addition to obtaining a knowledge of locomotives, it is essentia-that he should become fully acquainted with the Rules and Regulations which apply to him.

A study of the Permanent Notices and Rules 1 to 16 in the Rule Book will instruct him in his personal conduct and safety, and a knowledge of the following rules will prepare him for the time when he will be called upon to act as a Fireman :—

Rules Nos. 34-49	Fixed Signals
Rules Nos. 50-51	Hand Signals
Rules Nos. 55-56	Detention of Trains
Rules Nos. 126-8, 141-3	Working of Train
Rules Nos. 178-181	Protection of trains stopped by accident, etc.

He should have a knowledge of "Prevention of Accidents" as well as the proper procedure of coupling and uncoupling.

Cleaners

Before a Cleaner can be allowed to act as a Fireman he is required to show a satisfactory knowledge of the following subjects:—

    (i) General description of a locomotive, i.e. names and uses of principal component parts.

(ii) General knowledge of Rules and Regulations particularly applicable to:—
  Hand and fixed signalling.
  Protection of trains and opposite or other lines.
  Locomotive equipment.

(iii) Method of firing a locomotive, general duties and responsibilities of a fireman.

Examinations

A careful study of this Handbook will assist Firemen to become proficient in their duties and prepare them for their examination to pass as Drivers, which will be held on the following subjects:—

The technical examination to act as Driver, which will be carried out by a Motive Power Inspector, will comprise an oral and practical examination:—

(*a*) *Oral Examination*

The candidate to be examined in the following subjects:—

(i) Knowledge of locomotive.

(ii) Knowledge of mechanism of continuous brakes.

(iii) Method of dealing with locomotive defects.

(iv) Knowledge of rules and regulations.

(v) Knowledge of the various types of signals, their use and the rules relating to the reading of signals.

(vi) Knowledge of the making out of reports.

(*b*) *Practical Examinations*

The Examiner will give attention to the following points:—

(i) Care and manipulation of locomotive.

(ii) Attention to boiler and fire.

(iii) Attention to signals and judging distances.

(iv) Attention to rules and regulations.

(v) Knowledge of locomotive parts.

(vi) Making and using trimmings.

(vii) Care in and attention to oiling.

(viii) Examining locomotive and reporting defects.

(ix) General knowledge of automatic and steam brakes.

(x) Ability of examinee to change a boiler water gauge glass.

It must be clearly understood that the questions and answers printed in this book are not necessarily identical with those which will be asked at the examination.

ENGINEMEN'S DUTIES

Firemen

Good timekeeping is an essential part of a Railwayman's job. After signing on duty at the right time and reading the notices, the Fireman should then join his engine. His first duty is to examine the water gauges and notice the steam pressure. If the water level is satisfactory he should give attention to the fire, level it down and raise the steam pressure, to enable the injectors to be tested as early as possible.

He should satisfy himself that the fusible plugs and tubes are satisfactory and that the brick arch and firehole deflector plate and protection ring are in good condition, also the smokebox door is screwed up tight.

It is the Fireman's duty to draw tools and equipment from the Stores, where tools are locked up, and to clean and trim the lamps, where required to do so.

He must make sure that the required number of flags and detonators are carried and, where these are contained in a sealed canister, ensure that the seal is intact and the "date" indication correct.

Careful preparation of the fire is half the battle. He should start by spreading the fire over the grate evenly with a fire-iron, running this over the bars to clear the air spaces.

Some classes of coal require the use of broken firebrick, limestone or shingle, which prevents clinker adhering to the firebars. This must be thrown on the bars before spreading the fire.

The fire should be built up by adding small quantities of coal. Large coal must be broken to lumps little larger than a man's fist. This exposes to the action of the fire a greater surface of the fresh coal than would be the case if large pieces were used.

Firing should continue at intervals, giving each charge of coal time to ignite properly, until a bed of fire, well alight and suitable for the class of train to be worked, is obtained. The damper should be open and blower carefully applied sufficiently to avoid smoke.

He should be particular to sweep the front platform and the foot framing clear of all loose ashes and sand which would, if not removed, present an untidy and unkempt appearance, and, moreover, would blow into the motion and cause increased wear.

He should satisfy himself that the ashpan has been cleaned and that the dampers are in working order. The sand boxes must be filled, the fire-irons properly stowed and the coal safely stacked on the tender.

He should see that the cab, boiler fittings and tool boxes are kept clean; it must be remembered that a good Fireman takes a pride in the cleanliness of his footplate. When cleaning gauge glasses and protectors, he must make sure that the protectors are in good condition and that they are secured in the correct position. It is important that all pressure is released from the gauge glass before the protector is removed and that the protector is replaced before pressure is restored.

Any difficulties experienced or defects noted during preparation must immediately be brought to the notice of the Driver. The Driver is in charge of the locomotive and the Fireman's duties are carried out under the Driver's control and supervision.

Drivers

After signing on duty the Driver should read the current notices, sign for those which require it, and obtain his working instructions and any special instructions affecting his workings.

On arrival at the locomotive, the Driver should test the water gauges, satisfy himself that the fusible plugs and tubes are tight, note the condition of the fire and steam pressure, and see that the Fireman is correctly attending to his duties.

He should see both injectors tested and himself test the brake and sand gear, and, if any defects are observed, take steps immediately to have them remedied.

In making his examination and oiling of the locomotive, the Driver should have a definite system and always work to it. He should be acquainted with the differences in the layout of the various classes of engines with which he may have to deal in the course of his duties. By commencing at the same point, and always in the same order, he will deal with the various parts methodically.

The water pick-up gear, where fitted, should be tested and oiled and great care taken to see that the scoop is in the "UP" or "OUT" position and the handle secured to avoid any damage being done when the locomotive is moved.

When preparing a locomotive fitted with steam heating apparatus, during the carriage-warming season he should see that the flexible hosepipes and connections are in good order, the apparatus should then be tested by opening the cock at the tender end (or the cocks at each end on engines so fitted), next open the steam valve to discharge all condensation from the apparatus, close the cocks and see that the correct heating pressure can be obtained. If the regulation pressure cannot be obtained or is exceeded, the matter must be fully reported on a repair card and the defect remedied.

On engines fitted with rocking grates, drop grates or hopper ashpans the Driver should satisfy himself that the operating handle is in position, that the catches are secure and that the ashpan hopper doors are closed.

During the time an engine is being prepared, care must be taken to see that the safety precautions have been carried out and, before entering the motion, that the hand brake is hard on, the reversing gear in mid position and the drain cocks open in accordance with instructions contained in Permanent Notice B.R. 32709/1.

Working Trains

A Driver should have a thorough knowledge of the route over which the train is required to travel and have signed his Route Knowledge Card to this effect. If he is not fully conversant with any section he should obtain the services of a competent conductor.

The Driver must have with him on his engine a complete set of lamps, not less than 12 detonators and two red flags and such tools as may be prescribed by the Motive Power Superintendent. He is responsible for seeing that the prescribed lamps, etc., are exhibited and in good order and lighted when necessary. He must keep a good look-out when the engine is in motion, sound the engine whistle when necessary, especially as a warning to persons on the line and frequently when passing through tunnels, see that the proper signals are exhibited, observe and obey all signals, and all speed restrictions, have his Fireman disengaged when passing signalboxes, start his train carefully and proceed along the proper line, stop his train with care, paying particular attention to the state of the weather, the condition of the rails and the gradient as well as the length and weight of the train. During foggy weather he must keep a sharp look out for Fogsignalmen and when the signals cannot be seen assume that the signal is at caution or danger and proceed cautiously or stop immediately as the case may be. He must also observe the instructions contained in Rules 126 and 127 in addition to other instructions regarding the working of trains contained in the Book of Rules and Regulations, the General, Regional and Sectional Appendices and the Regulations for the working of the Vacuum Brake.

The Driver should always endeavour to operate the locomotive in the most efficient and economical manner consistent with the work to be performed by the use of the regulator and reversing gear.

His Fireman must, when not necessarily otherwise engaged, observe all signals and keep a good look-out all the time the engine is in motion. He must avoid waste of steam and water from injectors, strict attention being paid to the avoidance of unnecessary blowing off and creation of excessive smoke, and take care not to deposit engine ashes at other than the appointed places.

ENGINE DISPOSAL

Firemen

Towards the end of the run the fire must be levelled and worked down as low as possible to avoid arriving on the shed with a large amount of fire in the grate.

Upon arrival on the shed, and after reporting the arrival of the engine, coal will be taken and the tank filled with water, and the engine placed over the ashpit. After taking water the tank lid must be closed. Care must be taken during coaling to avoid spillage, and prevent damage to coaling apparatus by inadvertent movement of the engine.

On the ashpit the Fireman will, when required, empty the smokebox (locomotives fitted with self-cleaning smokeboxes will be dealt with in accordance with instructions). The fire will be withdrawn or cleaned as necessary and it is important to clear the ashpan thoroughly. Locomotives fitted with rocking grates and hopper ashpans will be dealt with in accordance with instructions posted at the Depot. Care must be taken to see that the hopper doors are left closed and secured and that the operating lever is replaced in position on the footplate.

It is essential to close the dampers and firehole door after the fire has been withdrawn, and the blower valve shut off to prevent the entry of cold air into the firebox, which would set up contraction stresses in the boiler plates, stays and tubes. (For the same reason the locomotive should, when necessary to move in own steam, be worked as lightly as possible to reduce the quantity of cold air which would be drawn through the empty firebox and tubes.)

The Fireman should collect, check and clean all tools and equipment for return to the stores or lock them up on locomotives where keys are provided. If any item has been lost or damaged he should inform the Driver, who will report the facts when signing off, and the Fireman should draw the Toolman's attention to the discrepancy when handing over the equipment.

Before leaving a locomotive after stabling, the boiler should be filled with water to a height of three-quarters of the gauge glass and the locomotive left secure with the hand brake hard on.

Drivers

Whilst the Fireman performs his disposal duties the Driver will make an examination of the locomotive; he should proceed systematically as when preparing and will book all known defects.

```
        Steam Railway Museum
             Kemble Drive
               Swindon
        Tel : 01793 466622
Date:           23May'02 16:01
Card Type:      Visa
Acct #:         4508232704772761
Exp Date:       04/03
Auth Code:      023844
Check:          2000
Server:         257 Alf
SALE
2659274                21084***
#2#020523
            A J.MR BUTLER

Subtotal:               19.99

Total:                  0    :

Please Sign Below

        /


Signature:.....................
Please Debit/Credit My Account
By The Total Indicated Above

CUSTOMER COPY
```

257 Alf

Chk 2000   23May'02 16:01   Gst

9780711006287
1 Hbk Rw St Loc En   19.99
4508232704772761
Visa   19.99

Retail   19.99
Payment   19.99

If necessary the Driver will make out a "Repair" card which should be written in ink or indelible pencil; it should be clearly filled in and as much detail as possible given concerning the defect. He should avoid reporting more than one item on one line of the card, each item to be clearly defined. He should be particular to report all blows and ascertain by test if necessary, during his examination, whence they originate.

He should note whether all valve spindles and piston rods and other points are properly lubricated, and examine all slide bar bolts, big and little ends, etc. Symptoms of defects noted whilst running should be properly reported. It must be borne in mind that the examining Fitter or the Fitter who will do the repair work may find the engine out of steam when he gets to it. The report should therefore convey to him as far as possible what is wrong so that he will be able to go straight to the defective part and not waste time examining parts that are working correctly.

If there are no known defects a "No Known Defects" card must be made out.

Before the locomotive is left, care must be taken to see that it is left secure with the regulator fully closed, reversing screw or lever in mid gear, cylinder cocks open, hand brake hard on and the blower valve closed.

Turning the Locomotive

An engine to be turned should always be taken on and off the turntable slowly and brought to rest easily to avoid straining the mechanism and the structure of the turntable. The competent Driver knows exactly where to stop, having previously noticed what part of that type of engine comes opposite a certain part of the turntable or to a landside mark as the case may be, so that he is able to stop quickly and easily in the desired position without waste of time re-setting. During the operation of turning, the hand brake must be screwed HARD ON, the reversing screw or lever in mid gear and the cylinder drain cocks opened.

Hand-operated turntables should always be pushed round and never pulled because, when pushing, the man operating the table is behind the bars so that if he should fall or slip the table will move away and leave him clear. A man pulling on the bar, however, might be injured if he slipped or fell because the bar would pass over him.

When operating a mechanically propelled turntable, in addition to the usual precautions taken to prevent movement of the engine, the propelling mechanism of the turntable must be handled carefully.

If of the vacuum tractor type, the starting valve must be opened slowly to minimise the shock to the gearing, care being taken to see that the catches are out before the tractor is started. The table must never be stopped by forcing the catches in. The tractor must never be used as a brake to stop the table by reversing. In all cases the tractor should be shut down at such a point that the table will roll to rest in the desired position of its own accord. The large ejector should always be used to create ample power to operate the tractor.

Enginemen called upon to work any kind of machinery must take certain elementary precautions in their own interest and that of others. They should take every opportunity to make themselves familiar with the different types of turntables and mechanised coaling plants and their controls.

A Fireman or a Passed Cleaner acting as a Fireman is under the control and supervision of the Driver upon whom falls the responsibility of assisting in training him in the early stages of his career. By tactful and careful instruction the driver, by recalling the time when he himself was in a similar position and acting on his own experiences, will have considerable influence which will reflect credit upon him, in addition to making each working day satisfying to both, in the knowledge of a job well done.

SECTION 2

COMBUSTION

Composition of Air and Coal

Combustion takes place when coal burns in air, and correct combustion can only be obtained by bringing together the right amounts of coal and air at the same time. To examine this statement more fully it is necessary that we should know something of the chemical constituents of coal and air.

Coal varies in quality and composition, but the greater part of it consists of carbon, the remainder being composed of gases and ash (see Fig. 1).

Air consists of a mixture by weight of approximately 23% oxygen and 77% nitrogen, or when measured by volume, 21% oxygen and 79% nitrogen.

Combustion is the chemical combination which takes place between the constituents of fuel and oxygen when the fuel burns. The heat-producing constituents of coal are carbon and hydrogen, heat being produced when these elements combine with the oxygen from the air. Coal must be heated to a temperature slightly above

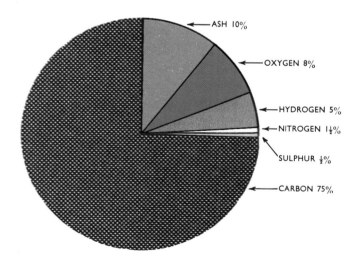

ASH 10%
OXYGEN 8%
HYDROGEN 5%
NITROGEN 1½%
SULPHUR ½%
CARBON 75%

Fig. 1 AVERAGE COAL CONSTITUENTS

800°F. before it commences to burn, but very much higher temperatures are necessary for it to burn efficiently.

Carbon and hydrogen are chemical elements and each requires a definite quantity of oxygen to burn it completely so as to obtain the maximum heat value. In this connection it is necessary for the carbon to combine with sufficient oxygen to form a colourless gas known as carbon dioxide, and for the hydrogen to combine with oxygen to form water vapour (steam).

If, however, the supply of air is insufficient, incomplete combustion results and another colourless gas called carbon monoxide is formed. In burning to carbon monoxide only about 30% of the heat is produced as there is when adequate air to burn the carbon completely to carbon dioxide is supplied.

> 1 lb. of carbon completely burned to carbon dioxide produces 14,550 British Thermal Heat Units (B.Th.U.s).

> 1 lb. of carbon incompletely burned to carbon monoxide produces only 4,350 B.Th.U.s, that is, about 70% of the heat is wasted.

Now we have already given particulars of the constituents of coal, but it must be clearly understood that these elements do not exist separately in the fuel. The actual composition is extremely complicated, but it is sufficient if we consider it as consisting of two main parts:—

> (1) Volatile (gaseous) matter, that portion which is given off as a gas when the coal is heated, and

> (2) Fixed (solid) carbon, in the form of coke, which remains behind after the volatile matter has been given off.

Volatile matter consists of numerous gaseous compounds of hydrogen and carbon known as hydro-carbons. These may be observed as yellowish smoke issuing from the chimney of a locomotive in which steam is being raised from cold, or when too many shovelfuls of coal are put on at one firing.

At high temperatures, in the neighbourhood of 2,500°F., the hydro-carbons split up into carbon and hydrogen and are burned to form carbon dioxide and water vapour, provided sufficient air is present. If, however, there is a shortage of oxygen some of the hydro-carbons escape up the chimney unburnt in the form of black smoke.

A normal Yorkshire steam coal contains about 33% by weight of volatile matter, and this contains practically all the hydrogen present in the fuel. This latter has a weight-for-weight heating value of approximately four times that of carbon.

> 1 lb. of hydrogen completely burned to water vapour gives off 62,100 B.Th.U.s of heat.

The sulphur content of coal is small and is of little consequence as a heat-producer. It is, however, usually found in the coal as a compound of iron known as iron pyrites. The sulphur burns out, leaving the iron, which at high temperatures tends to cause the ash to become welded together forming clinker.

Nitrogen in the coal is of no consequence. The nitrogen in the air required for combustion, however, plays a very important part in actual practice. A considerable volume of nitrogen has to pass through the firebox in the air required for combustion; 1 lb. of coal requires approximately 12 lb. of air for combustion of which 9 lb. are nitrogen. The nitrogen does not burn, but it does restrict the rate of combustion. Also, due to the fact that it has to be heated up by combusted gases in the firebox, it causes considerable loss of heat. The loss is due to the high temperature at which the gases leave the chimney, approximately 700°-750°F., and the loss due to this is, at a minimum, 10%.

What Happens in the Firebox

Let us now consider what takes place when coal burns in a locomotive firebox. Air is supplied to the firebox in two ways, viz.:—

(1) Primary air, through the firegrate, and

(2) Secondary air supplied through the firehole.

Assuming coal has just been fired on to an incandescent (white hot) firebed, the volatile gases commence to be given off at once from the newly added coal, and are quickly drawn out of the firebox and through the smoke-tubes, and unless sufficient air for complete combustion is made available they will pass out of the chimney-top in the form of dense smoke. Whilst the volatiles mix with a certain amount of primary air this will almost invariably be insufficient, and they will therefore depend upon adequate secondary air supply through the firehole door to enable proper combustion to take place.

As has been stated previously, the volatiles contain a large proportion of the heat value of the coal, and any failure to provide adequate air for combustion of these will result in considerable heat loss. The fixed carbon, which remains after the volatiles have been driven off, remains on the firebed until sufficient primary air is provided through the firegrate to burn it, and here again sufficient secondary air must be provided to ensure that the carbon is fully burned to form carbon dioxide.

Heat loss can also occur through admitting more air than is required for combustion: this excess air does not take part in combustion, and is heated up by the burning gases in the firebox, losses occurring due to the high temperature of discharge from the

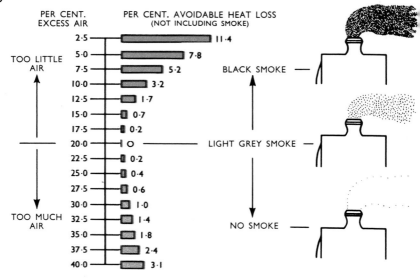

Fig. 2 EXCESS AIR, HEAT LOSS AND SMOKE

chimney in the same way as occurred with the nitrogen as described previously.

As a matter of interest, it is necessary to supply about 20% more air than is theoretically necessary to complete combustion in a locomotive firebox. If only the theoretically correct amount of air is supplied it is not possible to fully mix this with the combustible gases due to the high speed at which they are drawn through the firebox to the tubeplate, and losses occur due to incomplete combustion in consequence (see Fig. 2).

Principles of Good Firing

From the foregoing we have seen what conditions are required for efficient combustion; it is now necessary to see how proper combustion can be attained in actual practice.

On the road the art of firing is to regulate the fire and height of water in the boiler at all times according to the work to be performed and to have full boiler pressure when it is required, without blowing off.

Different types of coal require different handling, dependent upon their constituents. For example, a good-quality Welsh steam coal is very largely composed of fixed carbon and contains a comparatively small amount of volatile matter. Such coal requires a greater amount of primary air and less secondary air through the firehole door. On the other hand, a good-quality Yorkshire steam coal is proportionately high in volatile matter and requires considerably more secondary air.

Coal will be economically burnt when the firebed is of the right thickness. If the fire is too thick the air cannot pass through it. If the fire is too thin, excessive air passes through the firebed and holes will be formed. In both cases the firebox temperature will be considerably reduced.

As already pointed out, the volatile matter begins to be expelled from the coal immediately it is placed on the firebed. If too much coal is fired at one time the amount of volatile matter given off will be so great that it will be impossible to provide enough air to burn it completely. The amount given off must therefore be controlled so that it is no greater than that which the air supply can burn completely. This can be done by firing only a relatively small number of shovelfuls at one time.

The whole of the volatile matter is not given off immediately the coal is fired and it is therefore necessary to wait before firing again FOR A PERIOD LONG ENOUGH TO ENSURE THAT THE AIR SUPPLY CAN THEN BURN THE VOLATILE GASES STILL BEING RELEASED FROM THE FIREBED TOGETHER WITH THE LARGER AMOUNT WHICH WILL BE GIVEN OFF IMMEDIATELY THE NEW FIRING TAKES PLACE.

Volatile matter requires an extremely high temperature for proper combustion, and one of the purposes of the brick arch is to maintain this high temperature. It increases the length of the path the gases must travel and causes them to be rapidly ignited. The brick arch receives heat from flames and radiation from the firebed itself and, therefore, the fire must be kept at the highest possible temperature. This can be done by working with a fire no thicker than the minimum needed to produce a uniform firebed without holes. To keep the firebed at this thickness the coal must be fired at the same rate as it is being burned away.

To obtain the maximum amount of heat for the production of steam, the best method of firing is to limit the amount of coal put into the firebox at one time and to fire again only when the last charge of coal has burned away.

Although steam locomotives appear to work harder up rising gradients they also travel more slowly and so use little (if any) more steam in a given period of time than when working more easily but travelling faster on easy gradients. This means that because the demand for steam remains fairly constant all the time the regulator is open, there is no need to increase the rate of firing to any great extent when climbing gradients.

Fire sparingly—work systematically. This is the essence of good firing and has been proved conclusively, not only by tests but by analysing the way the best firemen work in practice on the road. No hard and fast rules can be laid down because locomotives vary as much as the work they perform and the men who man them. However, for the larger locomotives the best results are found in practice to be achieved by not exceeding 12 shovelfuls at one time and by firing no more often than is necessary for good combustion. Smaller locomotives need proportionately less at a time, but the actual rate of firing will be found by simple observation, for when too many shovels of coal are being persistently thrown into the firebox black smoke will result and the thickness of the firebed will increase excessively.

For all classes of locomotives the most common mistake is overfiring, whether by large amounts haphazardly fired or by small amounts fired too often. Not only is valuable coal wasted as a result, but the job is also made harder than it need be, because combustion is less efficient.

Preparing the Fire

First make sure that the water level in the boiler is correct and that every part of the firebars is free from clinker and ash by running the fire-iron along them if necessary and knocking dust through into the ashpan. When the coal is of a clinker-forming nature, place two or three shovels of broken fire-brick or limestone on the grate; when ash is forming this will prevent clinker from running over the firebars, restricting the air passage.

Build up the fire in stages: put on a layer of coal and let this burn through; then add another layer, until the depth of the firebed is correct for the work in hand. This method ensures that the fire is properly burnt through before starting. If steam is not immediately required, regulate the dampers; this will prevent (1) the fire burning up too quickly, (2) making smoke, and (3) blowing off.

Make sure that the ashpan is clean, the smokebox door is screwed up tight and the fire-irons and coal on the tender are secure. When the locomotive is prepared prior to working a train, arrange the boiler water level so that the injector can be applied to prevent blowing off at the safety valves without overfilling the boiler.

It is very important, before starting away from the shed, to examine the fire; if there are any hollow places, fill these up, if possible with hand-picked coal. Make sure that there are no air-holes or dead patches in the firebed and that the fire is burnt through all over the grate. NO METHOD OF FIRING CAN BE EXPECTED TO PRODUCE SATISFACTORY RESULTS IF THE FIRE IS IN POOR CONDITION AT THE START.

Starting Away with the Train

On no account should the locomotive be fired when starting away. At this time the temperatures of the firebed and brick arch are much lower than they will be at any other stage of the journey. The object now is to raise their temperatures as quickly as possible. This can best be achieved by partly closing the firehole door; by this means the greater part of the air flow, called primary air, passes through the firebed and raises its temperature. The amount of volatiles being given off by the fire at this stage is small on account of the low temperature, and therefore a large quantity of air over the firebed, that is, through the firehole door, called secondary air, is not necessary if the fire has been prepared properly. If the coal is put on the fire before it has reached a high temperature, it merely cools the fire, delays good steaming and wastes coal (see Figs. 3, 4A and 4B). After the train has travelled a little way and the driver has notched up the gear, that is the time to fire. The first shovelful should be placed where the fire is thinnest and if it is being pulled into holes, these should be filled up smartly; if there are patches which are not burning properly, miss them. Watch the chimney; if the fire is correct there will be in 15-20 seconds a light smoke at the chimney-top. When this light smoke has disappeared it will be time to fire again; the fire should be burning evenly all over the grate and the appropriate number of shovelfuls, according to the type of locomotive and work to be performed, should be added.

Firing on the Journey

After a few firings the fireman will prove for himself that the rate of firing need be no more than "little and often" and this also applies when the engine is climbing gradients. It is, of course, quite true that engines burn more coal *per mile* on rising gradients than when running on the level, but this does not mean the fireman should fill the firebox with heavy charges of coal at one time. In such cases the number of shovelfuls fired should not exceed one or two, certainly no more than two, over the number used on the level. Good team work by enginemen has a bearing on maintaining a good head of steam; this co-operation between the Driver and Fireman is most important with regard to economy in the use of coal.

An inefficient Fireman sometimes blames the Driver for using steam at an excessive rate; on the other hand, the Driver may charge the Fireman with mismanagement of the fire, allowing the boiler pressure to fall, and in order to keep scheduled time it is necessary for the Driver to increase the engine cut-off, thereby using more steam. If, therefore, the Fireman provides a satisfactory boiler

30

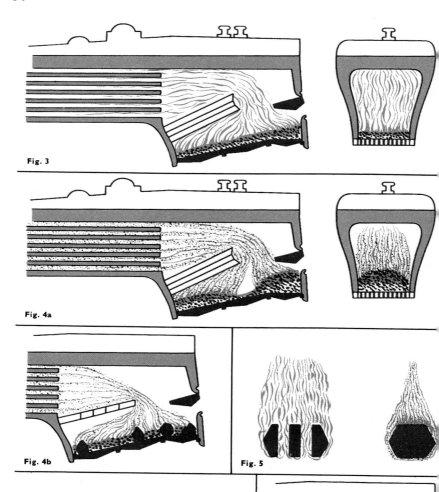

Fig. 3 CORRECT FIRE
Firebed with even surface; no air holes, hollow places or dead patches; every square foot of grate doing its job; combustion space above firebed full of intensely hot flames; combustion completed in firebox

Fig. 4a INCORRECT FIRE
Firebed uneven; air unable to flow through thick patches under door and front of brick arch; too much air flowing through hollow patch and up to the sides of the firebox causing gaps in flames; combustion not completed in firebox; thick black smoke produced

Fig. 4b INCORRECT FIRES
Large lumps of coal cause dead spots in firebed, gaps in flame stream and uneven firebed surface

Fig. 5 EFFECT OF SIZE OF COAL
Many more surfaces are exposed when a piece of coal is broken; smaller pieces will cover a bigger area of the grate than a single large lump and help to produce enough flame to fill the combustion space fully. Large coal should be broken down to about the size of a man's fist.

Fig. 6 INCORRECT POSITION OF BAFFLE PLATE
Baffle plate tilted up allowing air to pass direct to upper part of tubeplate, setting up strains, chilling nose of brick arch and laying foundations for dirty tubeplate and leaking tubes

pressure, the Driver, by skilful handling of the gear, can carry out the work in hand without having to resort to the use of excessive rates of steam consumption.

When the Regulator is Closed

When the regulator is closed on the journey, or about to be closed, no firing should be done. Also, toward the end of a run, the rate of firing can be decreased or stopped completely at some point which is found by experience to avoid arriving on the shed with too great a quantity of fire in the box.

When locomotives are standing in stations or sidings waiting to leave at an unexpected time the fire can be kept right by placing a few shovels of coal very occasionally, first at one part of the grate and then at another. In this way excessive smoke is prevented and the fire temperature can be raised quickly when required.

Blowbacks

When an engine is steaming normally a rate of burning is maintained which is proportional to the rate of steaming. Coal is consumed on the grate, and the gases produced are burnt above the fire in the secondary air stream which is drawn through the firehole door by the action of the exhaust steam passing through the blast pipe. This air stream can also be maintained by the action of the blower and it draws the flames and also the products of combustion towards the smokebox. If this air stream is interrupted, e.g. by closing the regulator, without opening the blower sufficiently, the combustible gases which are still being produced will be trapped in the firebox with two possible results:—

(a) Combustion may continue in the vicinity of the firehole door where air is still available. In these circumstances combustion will move towards this area, and flames will issue from the firehole door, producing what is known as a non-explosive blowback.

(b) Combustion may cease momentarily, and the gases then re-ignited from the firebed; this would produce an explosive blowback with very rapid flame propagation and possibly more serious results, due to flames entering the cab.

Contributory factors to blowbacks are:—

(a) Hard coals and some briquettes with their distinctive long flames.

(b) Black fires which produce more combustible gases than can be consumed.

(c) Running bunker or tender leading with the damper immediately below the firehole fully opened. Combustion in these circumstances tends to be much more rapid in the vicinity of the air intake below the grate resulting in the emission of gases and the presence of flame in the vicinity of the open firehole door.

(d) Low tunnels and bridges may momentarily arrest the normal direction of the air-gas stream.

(e) A plate of the self-cleaning smokebox arrangement falling across the blast pipe due to insecure fixing.

The following points should, therefore, be borne in mind in order to avoid incidents of this nature:—

(1) Avoid black fires by overfiring, which besides wasting fuel produce excessive quantities of combustible gases.

(2) Always open the blower before closing the regulator, and also when approaching low tunnels, deep cuttings or bridges, especially when using hard coal or briquettes.

(3) Avoid using the trailing damper when running bunker or tender leading.

(4) During preparation ensure that the self-cleaning equipment in the smokebox is securely fixed.

(5) When locomotives are working coupled together, and it is necessary to take water when passing over water troughs, the footplate staff in charge of the locomotive in the rear must take the additional precaution of seeing that the blower is open and the damper and firehole doors are in the closed position.

Firing of Shunting Locomotives

The working of these locomotives is intermittent in character, so that the demands for steam are varied; nevertheless, the rules of efficient firing still hold good. The general principle of "little and often" can best be applied by adding a few shovelfuls of coal at each time and firing as far as is practicably possible only whilst the engine is working.

Size of Coal

A large lump of coal, which when thrown on to the firebed protrudes above the general level, will burn more slowly than the rest of the bed and create a dead spot in the fire. Since maximum efficiency can only be achieved with an even firebed, such lumps should be broken up so that they will burn at the same rate as the rest of the bed (see Fig. 5). A good size to aim at is about that of a man's fist.

Use of Fire-irons

Firemen should avoid the use of fire-irons as far as possible. If the fire is caked, the fire-irons should only be used to break up the surface. If there is a good depth of fire when the ash and clinker are lifted up and mixed with the incandescent fuel, the ash will melt and run into the spaces between the firebars making things worse. If clinker has formed and it is necessary to break it up whilst running, the fire should be run down as low as possible and the clinker will then be much easier to break.

Use of Baffle Plate

The baffle plate placed in the firehole is designed to direct the air down towards the firebed in order to mix it thoroughly with the hot gases and flames.

If this plate is not in place, tilted upwards or burnt too short, cold air can pass over the nose of the brick arch to the upper section of the tubeplate, setting up considerable strains in these parts of the firebox, causing leaking tubes, dirty tubeplates and giving poor combustion (see Fig. 6).

Use of Dampers

The dampers control the flow of air through the ashpan to the firebed and they can be used to good effect to control the rate of burning under all conditions when the regulator is closed.

There can be no hard and fast rule as to which dampers should be used when the regulator is open on the journey; this depends upon the judgment of the Fireman.

Working of Injector

Both injectors should be tried before leaving the shed with the boiler pressure close to its maximum to ensure that they are in good working order, so saving anxiety on the run. When starting away with a train the water level in the boiler should be in sight at the top of the gauge glass. The injector can then be left off until the Fireman has fired a few times and the firebed and brick arch temperatures have been raised. When the water level drops to about $\frac{1}{2}$ in. from the top, the injector can be put on; the steam valve should be well open and the feed-water regulator pulled round towards the minimum, in order to ensure that the water enters the boiler at the highest possible temperature. The Fireman will then be doing all he can to keep up a constant feed to the boiler. The quantity of water put into the boiler should be equivalent to the amount of steam used by the engine. The injector feed should be adjusted to obtain these conditions.

SECTION 3

TRANSFORMATION OF
HEAT INTO POWER

The steam locomotive is a power plant in which there are four distinct divisions:—

(1) Fuel and combustion.
(2) Steam.
(3) Utilisation of steam.
(4) The driving mechanism.

Heat is a form of energy; therefore, when coal burns in the firebox of a locomotive its heat energy is capable of being expressed in terms of useful work. The high temperatures attained in the firebox by the combustion of the fuel varies according to conditions and may reach a maximum of 3,000°F. The heat so generated is transferred to the water in the boiler through the firebox plates and tubes, where it is converted to pressure energy in the form of steam, the steam in turn being led to the cylinders where it is transformed into mechanical energy and through the medium of the driving mechanism results in the tractive power of the locomotive.

British Thermal Unit

The production and utilisation of heat are the Fireman's chief concern; water and steam are only a means to an end—they bear the same relationship to a locomotive as does the harness to a horse that pulls the load. The state of the amount of heat or "hotness" in the firebox is measured by its temperature, and the unit of heat, in this country known as the British Thermal Unit (B.Th.U.), is 1/180th part of the heat required to raise the temperature of 1 lb. of water from freezing point to boiling point, i.e. 32° to 212°F., this being usually taken as the heat required to raise 1 lb. of water 1°F.

Methods of Heat Transfer

There are three methods by which heat may be conveyed from one body or place to another:—

Conduction:
Heat passes from one body to another by contact, warmer particles impart heat to the colder bodies. For example, boiler tubes transmit heat from the hot gases to the water through the metal by conduction.

Convection:

This is the transfer of heat by the hot gases in the firebox and by the circulating currents set up in the water, which takes the heat from the high-temperature parts. The moving hot gases in the firebox and circulating water in the boiler carry heat by convection to or from the metal surfaces with which they come in contact.

Radiation:

The fire in the firebox gives off energy in the form of radiant heat. Heat thus radiated to a body may be reflected, absorbed or transmitted. In the case of the firebox crown sheet the heat is absorbed by the metal, little being reflected, and the heat is then transmitted by conduction through the metal to the water.

Relation of Temperature to Pressures

When heat is applied to water to raise it to boiling temperature (212°F.), any additional heat will result in the water being transformed into steam at atmospheric pressure (14·7 lb. per sq. in.). Steam generated in a boiler, being enclosed, cannot escape, and if the application of heat is continued, more and more water is converted into steam which, being elastic, becomes compressed, decreases in volume and increases in pressure. As the pressure of steam on the surface of the water increases, so the temperature at which the water turns into steam rises correspondingly.

At atmospheric pressure (0 lb. per sq. in. on pressure gauge) 1 cu. in. of water when converted into steam occupies 1,642 cu. in. or nearly 1 cu. ft. At 15 lb. per sq. in. on the pressure gauge this steam will occupy only 821 cu. in., the pressure being doubled and the volume reduced by half. At 30 lb. per sq. in. the volume is only 410 cu. in., the steam being now compressed to one-fourth of its original volume. At 250 lb. per sq. in. the volume of 1 cu. in. of water converted into steam is only 110 cu. in.

Saturated Steam

The steam collected above the water in the boiler, termed "saturated steam", exerts an increasing pressure on its surface which resists the formation of the rising steam bubbles and calls for additional heat energy in the water. In short, the higher the pressure the greater the amount of heat required to create steam; for example:—

Steam at atmospheric pressure has a temperature of 212°F.
Steam at   85 lb. gauge pressure has a temperature of 327°F.
Steam at 225 lb. gauge pressure has a temperature of 397°F.
Steam at 250 lb. gauge pressure has a temperature of 405°F.

A table showing the range of steam pressure and temperature is given below:—

	STEAM PRESSURE-TEMPERATURE TABLE		
Gauge Pressure lb. per sq. in.	Temperature °F.	Gauge Pressure lb. per sq. in.	Temperature °F.
0	212·0	170	375·2
50	297·9	175	377·4
100	337·8	180	379·6
120	350·0	185	381·7
130	355·5	190	383·8
140	360·8	195	385·9
150	365·8	200	387·9
160	370·6	220	395·6
165	372·9	250	406·3

Superheating

Should the steam be further heated while in contact with the water from which it was generated, more water will be evaporated and the quantity of steam increased with an increase of temperature and pressure until the action of the safety valves prevents any further increase. On the other hand, if heat be added to the steam apart from the water from which it was generated, the steam becomes *superheated* and its temperature rises above that due to its pressure. The superheating of the steam is generally performed while the steam is no its passage from the regulator valve to the steam chest.

The temperature of superheated steam at working pressure ranges from about 600°F. to 750°F. depending upon the design of the superheater and the way in which the locomotive is being worked; in other words, the steam is heated about 300°F. above the saturated steam. The three main advantages of superheating the steam are that any entrained water in the saturated steam is converted into additional steam, cylinder condensation is prevented and the volume is increased as compared with saturated steam. This increase in volume is approximately 30% at a working pressure of 225 lb. per sq. in.; in consequence of this increase the demand upon the boiler to supply steam to the locomotive cylinders is considerably reduced, resulting in a saving in water and fuel.

The arrangements of the superheater and the utilisation of the expansive properties of the steam are described in subsequent sections.

SECTION 4

THE BOILER:
BOILER MOUNTINGS AND DETAILS

Types of Boilers and Fireboxes

The boiler or steam generator consists essentially of the steel shell, which includes the boiler barrel, the outer firebox wrapper plate, back plate, throat plate and smokebox tubeplate, also the inner firebox and the steel flue tubes. Fig. 7 shows a design of a boiler supplying saturated steam and Fig. 8 a boiler for supplying super-heated steam. The latter figure illustrates a taper boiler, the cylindrical barrel is made in two sections with the larger diameter at the rear, where the barrel is joined to the outer firebox. The dome in this design, which houses the regulator valve and auxiliary internal steam pipes, is positioned on top of the rear sloping section of the boiler barrel, where it forms a collector for steam above the surface of the water.

Fireboxes may be of the deep, long, narrow type between the frames or of the shallow, wide type, for example, as fitted to 4-6-2 classes of locomotives. In the latter case the firebox is spread over the frames. The wider type of firebox is generally employed when a large grate area is necessary.

The inner firebox is supported from the outer firebox by the foundation ring at the bottom, by crown stays at the top, and by palm stays between the firebox tubeplate and the boiler barrel. In addition, the firebox and outer wrapper plates, back plate and throat plate are stayed together with steel or copper stays, at about 4-in. pitch; there are over 1,000 of these stays in every locomotive boiler. Longitudinal stays are also fitted between the boiler back plate and smokebox tubeplate, and cross stays between the sides of the outer wrapper plate above the firebox crown. From the firebox tubeplate, the steel flue tubes, which may be anything from $1\frac{1}{2}$ in. to $2\frac{1}{4}$ in. diameter, pass through the boiler barrel to the smokebox tubeplate. When the boiler is fitted with a superheater, a number of large flue tubes (approximately 5 in. diameter) are provided in which super-heater elements are positioned.

Some boilers employ the flat-top type of firebox.

The boiler barrel and firebox are lagged with asbestos or glass wool.

It is normal practice in this country for inner fireboxes to be made

38

Fig. 7 SECTIONAL VIEW OF BOILER

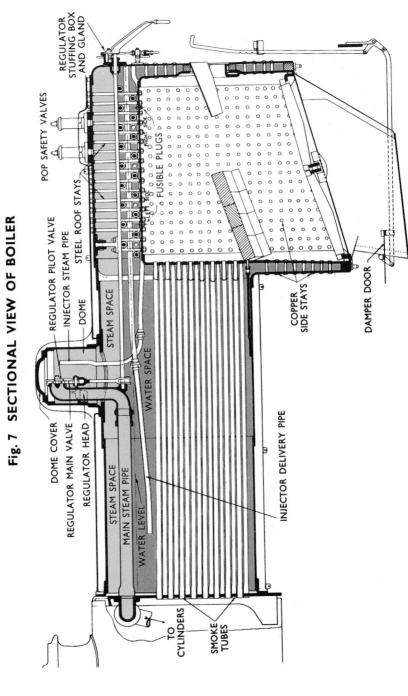

REGULATOR STUFFING BOX AND GLAND

POP SAFETY VALVES

REGULATOR PILOT VALVE

INJECTOR STEAM PIPE

STEEL ROOF STAYS

DOME

STEAM SPACE

RIGHT SIDE

LEFT SIDE

FUSIBLE PLUGS

COPPER SIDE STAYS

DAMPER DOOR

DOME COVER

REGULATOR MAIN VALVE

REGULATOR HEAD

STEAM SPACE

MAIN STEAM PIPE

WATER LEVEL

WATER SPACE

INJECTOR DELIVERY PIPE

TO CYLINDERS

SMOKE TUBES

Fig. 7

39

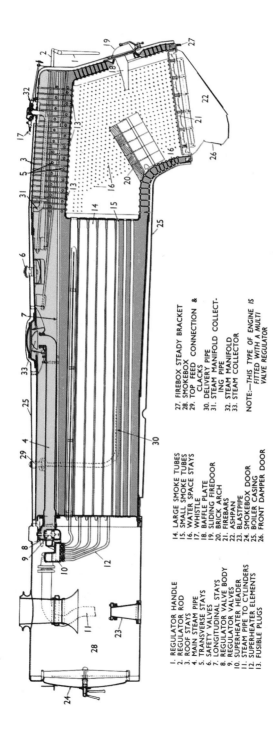

1. REGULATOR HANDLE
2. REGULATOR ROD
3. ROOF STAYS
4. MAIN STEAM PIPE
5. TRANSVERSE STAYS
6. SAFETY VALVES
7. LONGITUDINAL STAYS
8. REGULATOR VALVE BODY
9. REGULATOR VALVES
10. SUPERHEATER HEADER
11. STEAM PIPE TO CYLINDERS
12. SUPERHEATER ELEMENTS
13. FUSIBLE PLUGS

14. LARGE SMOKE TUBES
15. SMALL SMOKE TUBES
16. WATER SPACE STAYS
17. WHISTLE
18. BAFFLE PLATE
19. SLIDING FIREDOOR
20. BRICK ARCH
21. FIREBARS
22. ASHPAN
23. BLASTPIPE
24. SMOKEBOX DOOR
25. BOILER CASING
26. FRONT DAMPER DOOR

27. FIREBOX STEADY BRACKET
28. SMOKEBOX
29. TOP FEED CONNECTION & CLACKS
30. DELIVERY PIPE
31. STEAM MANIFOLD COLLECTING PIPE
32. STEAM MANIFOLD
33. STEAM COLLECTOR

NOTE:—THIS TYPE OF ENGINE IS FITTED WITH A MULTI VALVE REGULATOR

Fig. 8 SECTIONAL VIEW OF BOILER WITH SUPERHEATER

Fig. 8

of copper. The 4-6-2 type locomotives of the Southern Region (Merchant Navy and West Country classes) are, however, fitted with steel fireboxes and also with thermic syphons which increase the firebox evaporative surface and improve circulation in the boiler (see Fig. 9).

The Smokebox

The smokebox is an extension at the front end of the boiler barrel which, together with the blast pipe and chimney, forms the means of inducing air required for combustion to the firebox. Apart from the chimney orifice it is airtight. Other fittings in the smokebox are: superheater header (when fitted), main steam pipes, blower and ejector exhaust pipes. On some locomotives the regulator valve is situated in the superheater header in the smokebox (see Fig. 10).

Self-cleaning Smokebox

To avoid the accumulation of ashes in the smokebox, to even the effect of the blast over the whole tubeplate and to prevent emission of sparks thrown up the chimney, locomotives are now being fitted with self-cleaning type of smokebox (see Fig. 11). Deflecting and diaphragm plates with front spark arrester or ash plate are fitted. The vertical diaphragm plates, in front of the tubeplate, ensure that an equal draught passes through the tubes. The self-cleaning action is attained by locating the horizontal table plate just under the top flange of the blast pipe and setting the restriction plate at such an angle as, combined with sufficient area of netting, will allow for the free steaming of the locomotive. The diaphragm plates cause the ashes, drawn through the tubes, to traverse the lower part of the smokebox through the restricted opening "A" (Fig. 11); the ashes are then drawn through the wire net screen before being ejected through the chimney. By that time the ashes are small, dead and harmless.

The Superheater

The superheater consists of a steam collector or header for distributing steam from the boiler to a series of superheating tubes or elements and for receiving the superheated steam from the elements. The superheater header is attached by a flanged joint to the smokebox tubeplate at the outlet of the main internal steam pipe from the regulator valve and is placed horizontally across the upper part of the smokebox. At each side of the header are flanges to which are attached the main steam pipes to the cylinders (Fig. 9).

The header casting is divided into saturated and superheated compartments. Steam passing from the regulator valve to the main

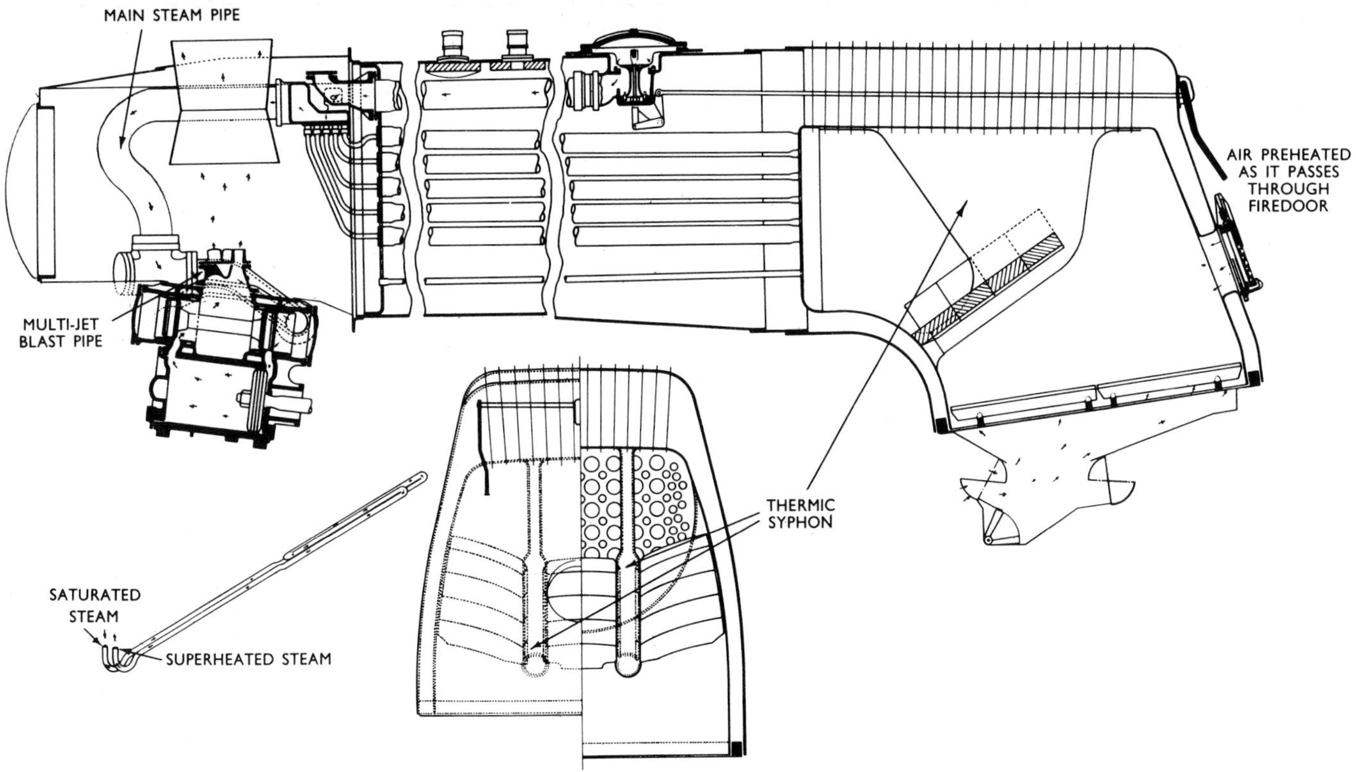

AIR PREHEATED AS IT PASSES THROUGH FIREDOOR

THERMIC SYPHON

MAIN STEAM PIPE

MULTI-JET BLAST PIPE

SATURATED STEAM

SUPERHEATED STEAM

Fig. 9   SECTIONAL VIEW OF BOILER WITH THERMIC SYPHON

Fig. 9

42

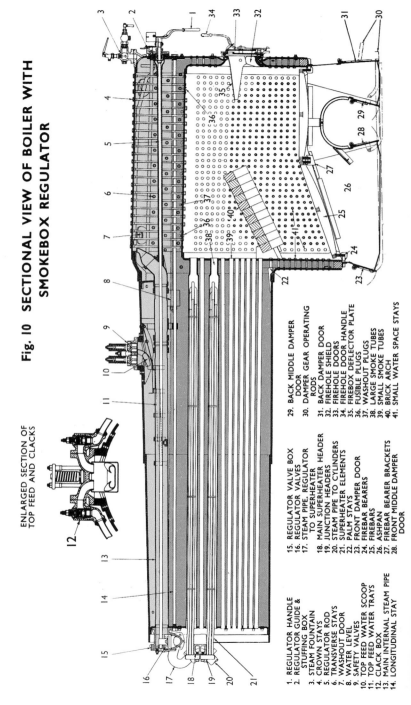

Fig. 10 SECTIONAL VIEW OF BOILER WITH SMOKEBOX REGULATOR

ENLARGED SECTION OF
TOP FEED AND CLACKS

1. REGULATOR HANDLE
2. REGULATOR GUIDE &
   STUFFING BOX
3. STEAM FOUNTAIN
4. CROWN STAYS
5. REGULATOR ROD
6. TRANSVERSE STAYS
7. WASHOUT DOOR
8. WATER LEVEL
9. SAFETY VALVES
10. TOP FEED WATER SCOOP
11. TOP FEED WATER TRAYS
12. CLACK BOX
13. MAIN INTERNAL STEAM PIPE
14. LONGITUDINAL STAY

15. REGULATOR VALVE BOX
16. REGULATOR VALVES
17. STEAM PIPE, REGULATOR
    TO SUPERHEATER
18. MAIN SUPERHEATER HEADER
19. JUNCTION HEADERS
20. STEAM PIPE TO CYLINDERS
21. SUPERHEATER ELEMENTS
22. PALM STAYS
23. FRONT DAMPER DOOR
24. FIREBAR BEARERS
25. FIREBARS
26. ASHPAN
27. FIREBAR BEARER BRACKETS
28. FRONT MIDDLE DAMPER
    DOOR

29. BACK MIDDLE DAMPER
    DOOR
30. DAMPER GEAR OPERATING
    RODS
31. BACK DAMPER DOOR
32. FIREHOLE SHIELD
33. FIREHOLE DOORS
34. FIREHOLE DOOR HANDLE
35. FIREBOX DEFLECTOR PLATE
36. FUSIBLE PLUGS
37. WASHOUT PLUGS
38. LARGE SMOKE TUBES
39. SMALL SMOKE TUBES
40. BRICK ARCH
41. SMALL WATER SPACE STAYS

Fig. 10

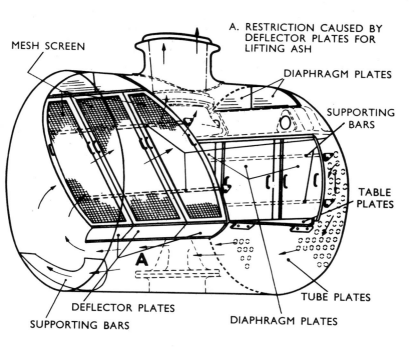

A. RESTRICTION CAUSED BY DEFLECTOR PLATES FOR LIFTING ASH

MESH SCREEN

DIAPHRAGM PLATES

SUPPORTING BARS

TABLE PLATES

TUBE PLATES

DEFLECTOR PLATES

SUPPORTING BARS

DIAPHRAGM PLATES

Fig. II   TYPICAL SELF-CLEANING SMOKEBOX

internal steam pipe can only reach the cylinders by traversing the superheater elements connecting the two compartments in the header, the elements forming the only communication between the two separate sections. On modern locomotives the number of superheater elements installed varies according to the size of the boiler and the degree of superheat required. The elements usually consist of continuous steel tubing of four lengths with three return bends, or of the bifurcated type with two return bends: the elements are positioned in large flue tubes which extend between the firebox and the smokebox tubeplates above the ordinary boiler tubes. Superheater flue tubes are from 5 in. to $5\frac{1}{2}$ in. diameter, reduced at one end for a distance of about 8 in. from the firebox tubeplate. The standard superheater element measures approximately $1\frac{3}{8}$ in. outside diameter and extends from the header in the smokebox to within a short distance of the firebox tubeplate, sufficient to avoid the element return bends coming in direct contact with the flames from the firebox.

The steam is superheated by the firebox gases flowing through the large flue tubes, giving up part of their heat to the steam passing through the elements when the regulator is open. The steam is first dried and then superheated. For example, steam at a pressure of 225 lb. per sq. in. and at a temperature of 397°F. enters the superheater header in a saturated state and, traversing the elements, returns to the header at a temperature of about 600°F., having been superheated by just over 200°F. and increased in volume by approximately 35%.

Blast Pipe

It has been stated in the section dealing with combustion that a large amount of air is necessary for efficient combustion in a locomotive firebox.

To supply the air, use is made of the exhaust steam from the cylinders in the following manner:—

Exhaust steam, after leaving the cylinders, passes through the exhaust passages to the blast pipe cap where it is slightly throttled so as to form a jet. The cap and the chimney are fixed on the same centre line and are suitably proportioned in relation to one another so that the escaping jet of exhaust steam, when passing through the chimney, carries with it the waste gases, thus creating a partial vacuum in the smokebox which induces the firebox gases to pass through the flue tubes and which, in turn, induces air to pass into the firebox through the grate and firehole door.

If the smokebox door is not airtight the vacuum will be reduced and bad steaming will result.

Whilst the majority of locomotives have a blast pipe cap of the fixed cone type, as described above, there are several variations. On ex-G.W.R. locomotives fitted with superheaters the "jumper"-type blast pipe cap is in extensive use.

It consists of a blast pipe cap fitted with a "jumper" ring and when the locomotive is working heavily the exhaust steam pressure lifts the jumper ring and provides an additional outlet for the exhaust, thereby reducing the tendency to lift the fire (see Fig. 12).

For this type of cap to fulfil its purpose it is most important that it should be kept clean and in good working order and the Fireman should brush away any accumulation around the top each day when he examines the smokebox. If the top is found defective it must be reported.

The double blast pipe cap comprises two fixed cone exhaust caps and requires two chimneys. The advantage of this design is that the

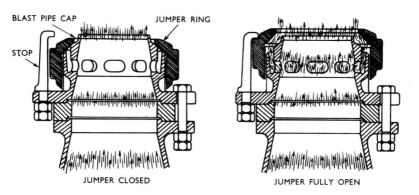

BLAST PIPE CAP

JUMPER RING

STOP

JUMPER CLOSED

JUMPER FULLY OPEN

Fig. 12 JUMPER BLAST PIPE TOP

same amount of draught can be induced with less exhaust pressure (see Fig. 13).

Many ex-S.R. express passenger locomotives are fitted with a multi-jet blast pipe cap which consists of five exhaust nozzles which

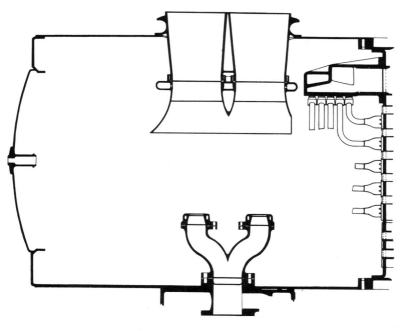

Fig. 13 ARRANGEMENT OF DOUBLE BLAST PIPE

exhaust through one large-diameter chimney (see Fig. 9); this has the same advantages as the double blast pipe.

Brick Arch

The brick arch is constructed within the firebox, abutting on the firebox on each side (Figs. 7 and 8). It extends from the tubeplate just clear of the bottom row of tubes and is inclined upward. Projecting into the firebox is the firehole door baffle or deflector plate, positioned so as to incline towards the arch from the firehole in a line slightly below the underside of the arch.

Firehole Doors

Various patterns of firehole door are fitted to locomotives ; these give access for firing and also can be adjusted to control the ingress of secondary air.

Drop Grates and Rocking Grates—Hopper Ashpan

Drop grates are fitted to facilitate disposal of the fire.

They are of varying types. One type consists of cast iron approximately 2 ft. × 1 ft 3 in., which forms part of the firegrate but which, being hinged, can be lowered to enable the clinker to be pushed through into the ashpan. On another type the drop grate forms the whole front section of the firegrate, as on some ex-L.N.E.R. locomotives.

Rocking grates are being fitted to B.R. standard types of locomotives. These consist of hinged firebars which can be rocked by means of levers in the cab (see Fig. 14).

A two-way stop and locking plate enables the grates to be operated with a limited amount of movement so as to break up the clinker when running, or to be rocked fully to enable the fire to be dropped at disposal. Care must be taken to see that the locking plate is in position during normal working.

With this type of grate a hopper ashpan is provided (see Fig. 15). This is fitted with bottom doors and is self-emptying when these are opened. The doors are held in position by a catch, and care should be taken to see that this and the locking key are secure after the doors have been closed tightly.

The hopper doors *should always be opened prior to dropping the fire during disposal* to prevent the hot fire damaging the ashpan, and these operations should only be carried out over a pit or other authorised cleaning point.

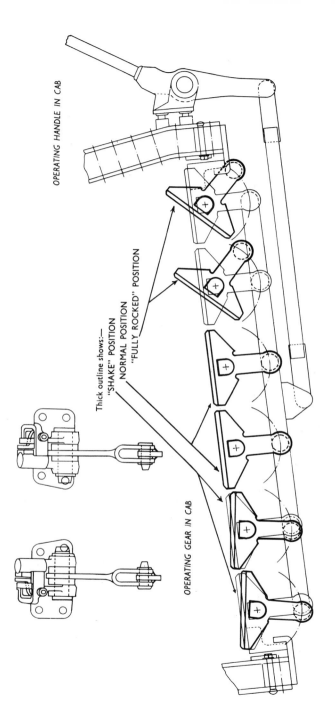

OPERATING HANDLE IN CAB

Thick outline shows:—
"SHAKE" POSITION
NORMAL POSITION
"FULLY ROCKED" POSITION

OPERATING GEAR IN CAB

Fig. 14 ARRANGEMENT OF ROCKING GRATE

Fig. 14

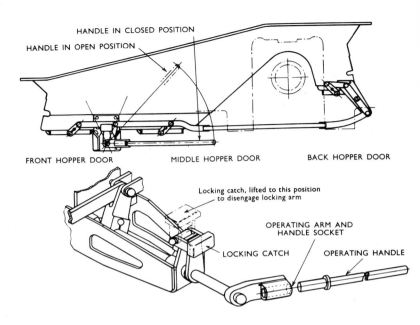

HANDLE IN CLOSED POSITION

HANDLE IN OPEN POSITION

FRONT HOPPER DOOR MIDDLE HOPPER DOOR BACK HOPPER DOOR

Locking catch, lifted to this position
to disengage locking arm

OPERATING ARM AND
HANDLE SOCKET

LOCKING CATCH OPERATING HANDLE

Fig. 15 ARRANGEMENT OF HOPPER ASHPAN

Boiler Mountings and Steam-using Auxiliaries

The boiler mountings and steam-using auxiliaries necessary for the efficient and safe working of locomotives are as follows:—

1. Safety valves.
2. Water gauges.
3. Pressure gauge.
4. Fusible plugs.
5. Injectors and clacks.
6. Regulator valve.
7. Washout plugs, hand hole and mudhole covers.
8. Blower valve and ring.

Safety Valves

Safety valves are fitted to prevent the boiler pressure from exceeding the registered working pressure of the boiler which is the steam pressure for which it was designed and is indicated by a metal tablet secured to the firebox back plate.

If the pressure at which the safety valves commence to blow off differs more than 5 lb. per sq. in. from the registered boiler pressure, this fact must be reported on a "Repair" card.

The "Pop"-type safety valve is in extensive use on British Railways (see Fig. 16).

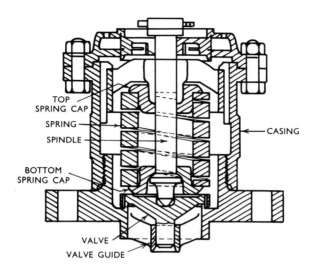

Fig. 16 SAFETY VALVE

In this design, when the working pressure is reached, the spring-loaded valve rises and admits small amounts of steam through a lip on the valve to the annular chamber, and this escapes through the holes in the top cap of the valve.

The steam, when escaping, acts on the increased area of the top cap and adds to the force already keeping the valve off its seating until such time as the pressure in the boiler has dropped slightly. The spring then overcomes the pressure of the escaping steam and the valve is instantaneously closed.

Blowing off can be avoided by careful management of the fire and injectors. On a modern 4-6-0 locomotive with a tractive effort in the neighbourhood of 26,000 lb. there is a loss of pressure and wastage of approximately 10 gallons of water for each minute the safety valves are open.

Water Gauges

Water gauges are mounted on the boiler back plate in the cab of the locomotive and are positioned so that when the water is in sight

Fig. 17 WATER GAUGE

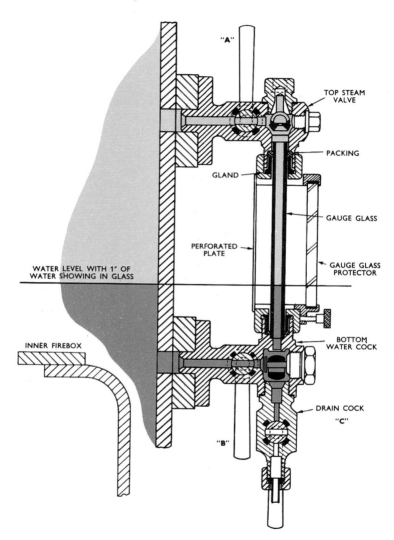

TO TEST GAUGE COCKS

1. Shut top cock and bottom cock by pulling handles **A** and **B** backwards until horizontal
2. Open drain cock by pulling handle **C** backwards until horizontal and water should disappear
3. Blow through top cock by opening with handle **A** and close again
4. Blow through bottom cock by opening with handle **B** and close again
5. Shut drain cock with handle **C**
6. Open top cock and bottom cock with handles **A** and **B** and water should rise to level

TO TEST GAUGE COCKS

1. Shut top and bottom cocks by pulling handle **A** until it is pointing downwards halfway between the horizontal and vertical

2. Open drain cock by pulling handle **B** upwards until horizontal, and water should disappear

3. Open top and bottom cocks by raising handle **A** slowly until it is pointing upwards halfway between the horizontal and vertical in order to blow through, and close again

4. Shut drain cock by turning handle **B** downwards

5. Open top and bottom cocks with handle **A** until it is pointing upwards halfway between the horizontal and vertical and water should rise to level

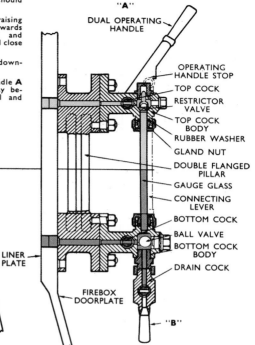

Fig. 18 WATER GAUGE
TOP AND BOTTOM COCKS COUPLED

at the bottom of the glass, the firebox crown is covered.

When working under normal conditions the water should be kept in sight in the top half of the glass, and before descending severe gradients or working over curves with a large amount of super-elevation a higher water level should be carried.

Normal running with too high a water level is detrimental to efficient locomotive performance in that a larger amount of water is carried over with the steam and the risk of priming is increased.

Types of water gauges are shown in Figs. 17, 18 and 19.

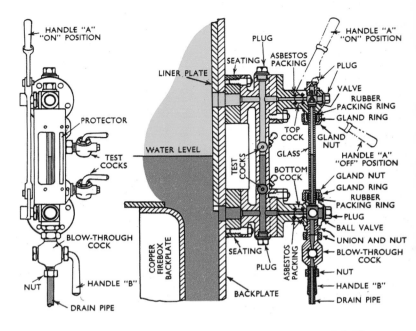

Fig. 19 WATER GAUGE WITH TEST COCKS

Pressure Gauge

The essential element of the pressure gauge is the Bourdon tube, connected by mechanism to a finger which indicates the pressure of steam in the boiler. The tube, usually made of phosphor bronze, is of oval cross-section and bent in the form of an arc of a circle, having one end fixed to a block which has a screw connection to the steam gauge pipe. The other end of the tube is sealed and is connected by a rod and pinion which magnifies the movement.

When pressure is applied, the tube tends to straighten out and the free end lifts by an amount proportional to the pressure applied by the steam.

Similarly, if a vacuum or negative pressure is applied the tube tends to close up and the pointer moves in the reverse direction as in a vacuum gauge.

Fusible Plugs

One or more fusible plugs are screwed into the firebox crown. These are of brass; some have a lead core which melts at a comparatively low temperature, and others have a brass button, secured by a lead filling.

If the water level in the boiler drops too low and uncovers the plugs, the lead melts and allows steam to escape into the firebox, which acts as a warning to the Enginemen. Should this occur both injectors should be immediately put on and steps taken to remove or deaden the fire.

Washout Plugs, Handhole and Mudhole Doors

These are fitted to facilitate periodical inspection and cleaning of the boiler water spaces.

Blower and Valve

The blower consists of a perforated ring fitted round the top of the blast pipe cap or, alternatively, cast integral with the base of the chimney, the steam supply being controlled from a valve on the footplate.

Its function is to create a smokebox vacuum for the following purposes:—

(a) To increase the draught on the fire when the locomotive is stationary in order to raise steam pressure.

(b) To clear smoke.

(c) To counteract back draught.

(d) To supplement the blast, if necessary.

In the case of (c), whilst working a train or light engine, the blower valve must always be opened prior to closing the regulator, also before entering a tunnel, and when passing over water troughs should be used as a further precaution to closing the ashpan dampers and firehole door.

Regulator Valves

Regulator valves of the vertical slide, horizontal slide balanced circular and double-beat types as well as the multiple-valve type in the superheater header are in common use on British Railways.

Vertical Slide-type Regulator

A typical vertical slide type is positioned in the dome as shown in Fig. 20. The regulator head usually has four ports, two small for starting purposes and two large size for normal running. The main valve, which has four ports, slides on its seating on the regulator head, and the pilot valve in turn seats upon the main valve, being held in position by a flat spring.

The first movement of the regulator handle lifts the pilot valve until the small ports are open. Further movement of the handle

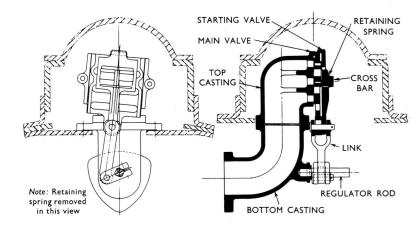

Fig. 20 REGULATOR VALVE VERTICAL DOME TYPE

moves both the pilot valve and the main valve together, which action opens the large ports and closes the starting ports. During closing, the pilot valve is first moved over the main valve to its normal closed position and then both valves are brought back together to their original position, closing the steam ports as they come down.

The independent movement of the pilot valve is obtained by the use of an elongated hole or slot in the main valve, the result being that the latter does not move until the pin has travelled a distance corresponding to the clearance of the slotted hole, a distance which is equal to the lap and port opening of the valve.

The pilot valve is provided to allow a gradual admission of steam into the main steam pipe so as to balance the pressure on the main valve, thus making easy and accurate adjustment possible.

Horizontal Dome-type Regulator

The horizontal slide dome type of regulator is shown in Fig. 21. It is similar in principle to the vertical pattern.

A main valve and pilot valve are employed, but the operating pin engages with slots formed in the raised sides of the valves. The slots in the main valve are wider than the diameter of the pin by an amount equal to the lap plus the port opening of the pilot valve.

Horizontal Regulator Smokebox Type

This regulator employs main and pilot valves similar to those of the dome type, but is positioned in the smokebox (see Fig. 10).

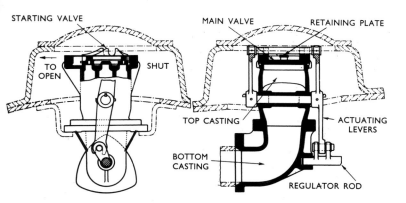

Fig. 21 REGULATOR VALVE HORIZONTAL DOME TYPE

Double-beat Type Regulator

The double-beat type of regulator valve is shown in Fig. 22.

This valve is mounted on a vertical cast-iron pipe in the dome. The valve is double, there being really two valves cast in one with two corresponding seats in the regulator head.

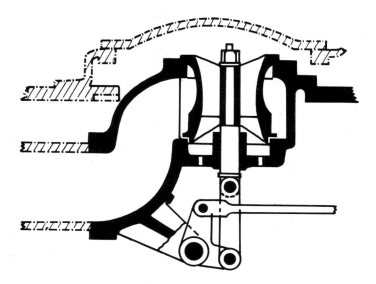

Fig. 22 DOUBLE-BEAT-TYPE REGULATOR VALVE

Steam is admitted past both top and bottom seatings simultaneously when the valve is opened, entering the lower seat by passing through the centre of the valve. In some designs the upper seat is somewhat larger than the lower seat to allow it to be placed in the head and, this slight difference in area between the top and bottom seats has the advantage of ensuring that the valve will move into the closed position should any connection break.

Multiple Valve Regulator

In this type of regulator a number of valves situated in the superheater header open in turn as the regulator handle is moved; the object is to obtain fine regulation of the steam flow with a minimum of effort to operate the regulator.

Injectors

The injector is an appliance for delivering feed water to a boiler. In its simplest form it embodies three essential cones, the "steam cone", the "combining cone" and the "delivery cone". The steam cone admits the steam to the injector, guides it in the direction in which it should flow, and limits, by its bore, the amount of steam passing through. Steam leaving this cone comes in contact with the water, is condensed by it and passes into the combining cone (Fig. 23).

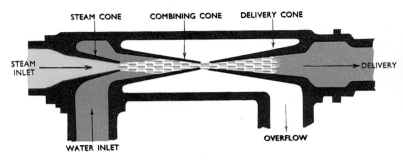

STEAM CONE   COMBINING CONE   DELIVERY CONE

STEAM INLET

DELIVERY

WATER INLET

OVERFLOW

Fig. 23 SIMPLE INJECTOR

When steam is allowed to expand in the steam cone from a higher to a lower pressure a certain amount of heat is available for conversion into work and this is spent in giving velocity to the steam itself in the direction of its flow.

The first point to remember, therefore, is that the change from pressure energy to velocity energy is brought about in the steam cone.

In the second or combining cone the slowly moving water combines with the swiftly moving steam, and the function of this cone is to ensure that the steam jet is condensed by the water. The cooler the feed water the better is the condensation of the steam. The combining cone is convergent in shape, the bore of the cone decreasing, with the result that the jet consists at its inlet end of a mixture of steam and water and at the outlet end of a solid jet of hot water flowing with high velocity into the delivery cone. Between the combining and the delivery cone is a gap, known as the overflow gap, through which excess steam and water are by-passed during the starting operation.

The second point to remember is that the combining cone effects the complete combination of the steam and water into the solid jet by the condensation of the steam and the transference of its energy to the water.

The delivery cone is so constructed that the change from velocity to pressure energy takes place as uniformly as possible. The momentum of the jet, which is greatest at the choke or smallest diameter of the delivery cone, is gradually reduced in velocity and increased in pressure sufficient to overcome the boiler pressure on the top of the clack valve. The temperature of the water is usually increased about 100°F. in passing through the injector. The size of an injector is determined by the throat or smallest diameter of the delivery cone, this dimension being stated in millimetres (mm.).

The third point to remember, therefore, is that the function of the delivery cone is to convert the velocity energy of the combined jet into pressure energy.

The early injectors described proved difficult to start and unreliable when used on locomotives, due to vibration, set up whilst running, affecting the combined jet of water and steam in its passage from the combining cone to the delivery cone. Modern injectors are designed to overcome this difficulty and automatically restart should they inadvertently "knock off".

Fig. 24 shows a design of an injector which has been adopted as standard for British Railways.

The injector works in exactly the same manner as described previously, i.e. a jet of steam emerging at high velocity from the steam cone is brought into contact with the cold feed water which surrounds the tip of the steam cone and is partially condensed, causing a partial vacuum. This in turn causes the water to be drawn forward at a considerable speed into the combining cone. Passage through this completes the condensation of the steam and at the same time it releases its velocity energy to the water which is forced

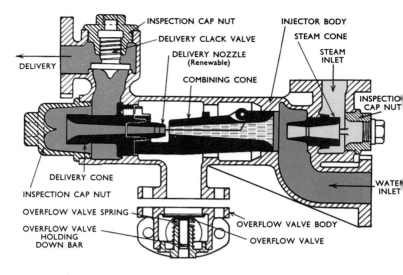

Fig. 24 INJECTOR COMBINING CONE WITH HINGED FLAP

forward at considerable speed through the small end of the cone. The water jet then jumps the overflow gap and enters a diverging delivery cone where the speed of flow and velocity energy, on its passage through the cone, exceeds the boiler pressure sufficiently to enable the feed water to lift the clack valve and enter the boiler. The upper portion of the combining cone is formed by a hinged flap and the vacuum developed in the combining cone, when the injector is working, holds this flap against the fixed portion which then forms a continuous cone. If the action of the injector is interrupted or the water jet upset, the vacuum in this cone is replaced by a pressure which forces the hinged flap open, allowing any surplus steam and water to escape through the gap so formed to the overflow outlet. When the pressure has thus been relieved the working vacuum rapidly re-establishes itself and the injector will then start again.

Fig. 25 shows a type of injector which is fitted to large numbers of locomotives; in this arrangement the combining cone has a fixed and movable portion. In this arrangement the steam, during its passage along with the feed water through the combining cone, is fully condensed, causing a high vacuum which holds the movable portion of the cone in contact with the fixed portion, forming in effect one continuous cone; if, however, the action of the injector is interrupted or the water jet upset, the vacuum in the cone is replaced

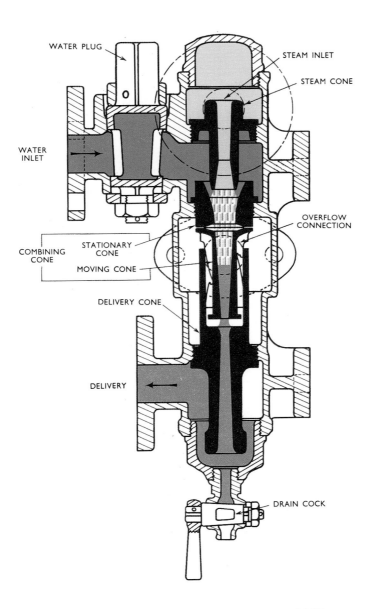

**Fig. 25 INJECTOR COMBINING CONE
FITTED WITH MOVABLE PORTION**

Fig. 26 LIVE STEAM INJECTOR MONITOR TYPE

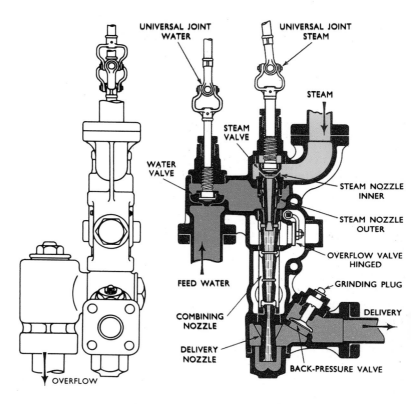

UNIVERSAL JOINT
WATER

UNIVERSAL JOINT
STEAM

STEAM

STEAM
VALVE

WATER
VALVE

STEAM NOZZLE
INNER

STEAM NOZZLE
OUTER

OVERFLOW VALVE
HINGED

FEED WATER

GRINDING PLUG

DELIVERY

COMBINING
NOZZLE

DELIVERY
NOZZLE

BACK-PRESSURE VALVE

OVERFLOW

WORKING INSTRUCTIONS

To Start: Open water valve, then steam valve fully
To Shut Off: Close steam valve, then water valve
Regulate for quantity with water valve

by pressure causing the movable cone to leave its seating, thus allowing any surplus water and steam to escape through the overflow.

When the pressure has been relieved the working vacuum is quickly re-established and the injector will re-start, the movable portion of the combining cone having again taken up its normal working position.

One of the latest types of injectors is the "Monitor" type, as shown in Fig. 26 ; in this arrangement it will be noted that there are two steam cones and that the combining cone is without moving parts, but is fitted with slots. When the water cock is opened, the water flows into the combining cone and passes through the slots to the overflow; when steam is turned on it is directed in two jets, first the primary annular jet, and second, the secondary forcing jet. The primary jet, on leaving the steam cone, comes into contact with the feed water and forces it down the combining cone past the end of the inner steam cone at which point the second jet of steam is introduced, giving further impulse to the combined jet.

The combined jet flows through the combining cone where condensation is completed and then enters the delivery cone.

Should interruption take place causing the injector to "knock off", the steam and water escape freely through the combining cone slots to the overflow until the jet is reformed by the condensation of the steam and the injector restarts.

Exhaust Injectors

Exhaust injectors provide an economical method of injecting water into the boiler by utilising a small amount of exhaust steam from the cylinder for this purpose. Exhaust steam which would otherwise go to waste also heats the feed water, so that a hot delivery to the boiler is obtained; therefore, for most economical results the injector should be at work when the regulator is open, the feed being regulated by the water regulator handle on the Fireman's side of the cab.

The "H", "J", "H/J" and "K" types of exhaust injector are shown in Figs. 27, 27A, 28, 28A and 29.

When the regulator is open the injector works with exhaust steam in conjunction with a supply of supplementary live steam. With the regulator closed, additional auxiliary live steam is necessary to take the place of the exhaust steam.

On all four types of exhaust injector mentioned the changeover from exhaust to auxiliary live steam is provided automatically, being governed by the pressure in the steam chest. Earlier types do not have the automatic control.

Steam-controlled Exhaust Steam Valve

When the locomotive is at work with regulator open, the exhaust steam valves in the injector are open, admitting exhaust steam to the injector; but if the injector is not in use or when the regulator is closed, the exhaust steam valves are automatically shut.

Auxiliary Shuttle Valve

This valve automatically controls the admission of steam to the injector, either exhaust steam or auxiliary live steam, according to

Fig. 27 EXHAUST INJECTOR ARRANGEMENT AND CONTROL CLASS "H"

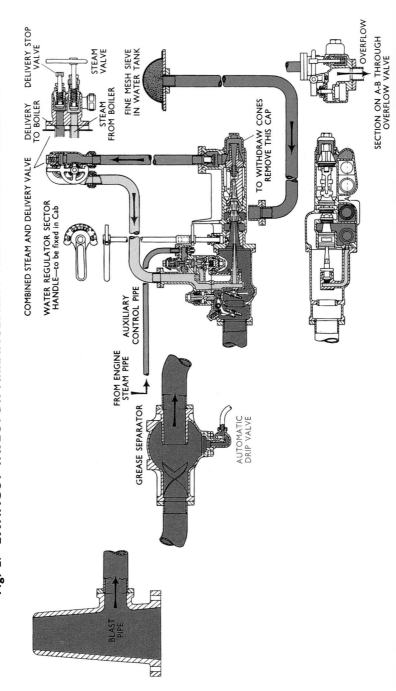

COMBINED STEAM AND DELIVERY VALVE

DELIVERY STOP VALVE

DELIVERY TO BOILER

STEAM VALVE

STEAM FROM BOILER

FINE MESH SIEVE IN WATER TANK

OVERFLOW

SECTION ON A–B THROUGH OVERFLOW VALVE

TO WITHDRAW CONES REMOVE THIS CAP

WATER REGULATOR SECTOR HANDLE—to be fixed in Cab

AUXILIARY CONTROL PIPE

FROM ENGINE STEAM PIPE

GREASE SEPARATOR

AUTOMATIC DRIP VALVE

BLAST PIPE

Fig. 27

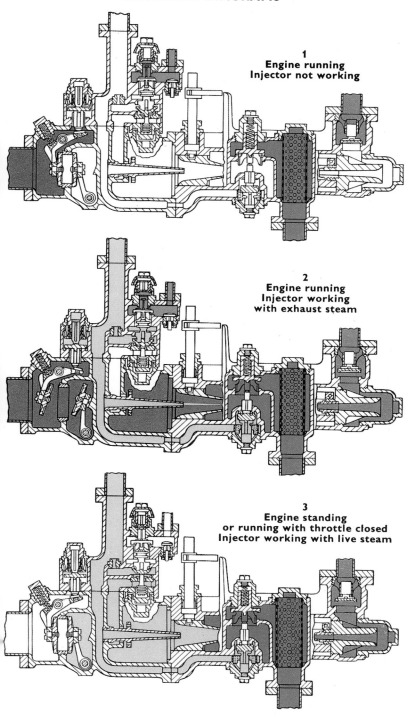

1
Engine running
Injector not working

2
Engine running
Injector working
with exhaust steam

3
Engine standing
or running with throttle closed
Injector working with live steam

64

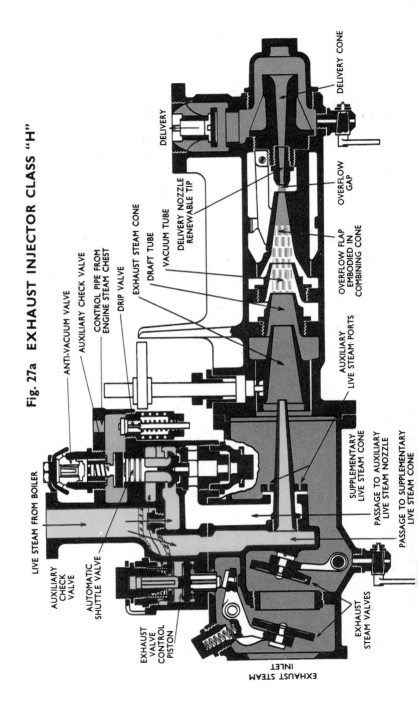

Fig. 27a **EXHAUST INJECTOR CLASS "H"**

DELIVERY CONE

DELIVERY

ANTI-VACUUM VALVE

AUXILIARY CHECK VALVE

CONTROL PIPE FROM ENGINE STEAM CHEST

DRIP VALVE

EXHAUST STEAM CONE

DRAFT TUBE

VACUUM TUBE

DELIVERY NOZZLE RENEWABLE TIP

OVERFLOW GAP

OVERFLOW FLAP EMBODIED IN COMBINING CONE

AUXILIARY LIVE STEAM PORTS

SUPPLEMENTARY LIVE STEAM CONE

PASSAGE TO AUXILIARY LIVE STEAM NOZZLE

PASSAGE TO SUPPLEMENTARY LIVE STEAM CONE

EXHAUST STEAM VALVES

LIVE STEAM FROM BOILER

AUXILIARY CHECK VALVE

AUTOMATIC SHUTTLE VALVE

EXHAUST VALVE CONTROL PISTON

EXHAUST STEAM INLET

Fig. 27a

whether the regulator is open or closed. When the regulator is open and exhaust steam available the auxiliary live steam is shut off, but when the regulator is closed and exhaust steam is not available, this is automatically replaced by a supply of live steam through the action of the shuttle valve controlling the supply of steam to the auxiliary live steam nozzle.

Steam-controlled Water Valve

The water valve is always in the shut position when the injector is not in use, but automatically opens immediately the steam valve is opened to start the injector.

The "J"-type exhaust injector differs from the "H" type in the following: the two pivoted exhaust steam valves in the "H" type are replaced in the "J" type by a double-beat spring-loaded valve fitted vertically and controlled by a steam piston below the valves. The automatic shuttle valve or change-over valve, is fitted below the "J"-type injector with the addition of an automatic choke valve to regulate the quantity of auxiliary steam supplied to the injector when the regulator valve is shut. In the "J" type the automatic water control valve has been replaced by a manual-operated disc water valve on the body of the injector or above the water entrance to the nozzles. This disc valve is fitted directly on to and worked by the water regulator spindle and rotated by it. The water valve merely acts as a water admission valve and does not regulate the quantity of water admitted to the injector cones, which is controlled by the movable exhaust steam cone as in the "H"-type injector. To shut off the "J"-type injector the steam valve is closed and the water regulator spindle moved to the shut position. In the "H/J" type the automatic water valve as on the "H" type is fitted to what is otherwise a "J" type injector.

The "K" type of exhaust injector is the latest design to be introduced and is fitted to the larger B.R. standard design of M.T. tender locomotives. In this design the movable exhaust steam cone, which has previously been used to control the amount of water delivered by the injector, has been replaced by a fixed exhaust steam cone and the water supply controlled by a variable water valve which is separate from the exhaust injector body but connected to it by an intermediate feed-water pipe. This arrangement enables both the injector and the water valve to be placed in accessible and convenient positions.

The "K"-type combining cone differs slightly from the previous designs in that in addition to the hinged overflow flap there are two overflow slots.

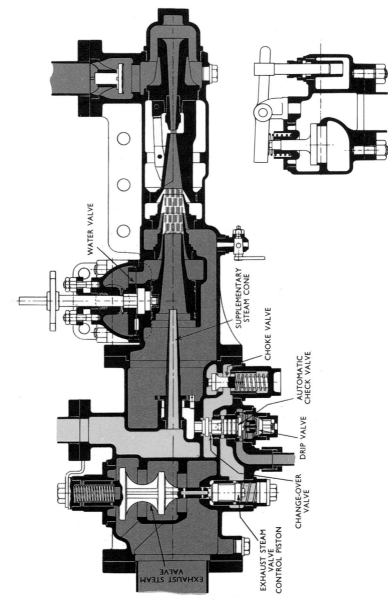

Fig. 28 EXHAUST INJECTOR CLASS "J"

WATER VALVE

SUPPLEMENTARY STEAM CONE

CHOKE VALVE

AUTOMATIC CHECK VALVE

DRIP VALVE

CHANGE-OVER VALVE

EXHAUST STEAM VALVE CONTROL PISTON

EXHAUST STEAM VALVE

OVERFLOW

Fig. 28

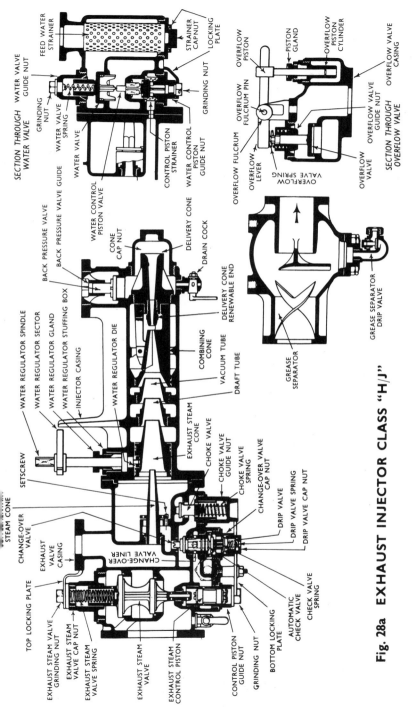

Fig. 28a   EXHAUST INJECTOR CLASS "H/J"

SECTION THROUGH
WATER VALVE

SECTION THROUGH
OVERFLOW VALVE

Fig. 28a

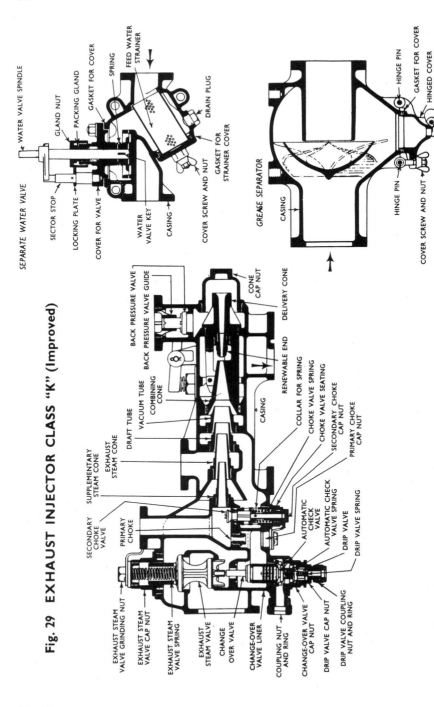

Fig. 29 EXHAUST INJECTOR CLASS "K" (Improved)

Fig. 29

Possible Causes of Injector Failures

(a) Dirt or scale on the injector cones or excessive wear or distortion of the cones.

(b) Air leaks in water supply. Air drawn in with the feed water causing bubbles which break up the jet.

(c) Insufficient feed water supply owing to an obstruction in the tank sieve (as a preventative keep tank lid closed to prevent entry of foreign matter); supply valve not properly open or tender tank empty.

(d) Feed water too hot.

(e) Choked delivery pipe, due to scale.

(f) Clack not seating properly.

(g) Defect in connections to coal watering pipe.

(h) Some of these defects may allow the injector to work intermittently or at certain pressures only. Full details of the irregularity should be properly described on the "Repair" card for the guidance of Fitters, bearing in mind that it is not always easy to test an engine over its full range of working conditions when the locomotive is stabled in the shed.

There are few things more annoying to Enginemen than an injector which misbehaves on the journey; it is therefore policy to make a practice of using both injectors in turn where two live steam injectors are fitted. Where an exhaust injector is provided, this should not be used during shunting operations when the regulator is being continually opened and closed in order to avoid undue wear to the change-over valve and risk of scalding staff on the ground.

Blowdown Valves

Softened water for locomotive purposes is provided extensively in some areas of British Railways to reduce scaling and corrosion in boilers. In connection with this continuous blowdown valves are fitted to locomotives so that a small measured quantity of water is drained from the boiler continuously, (1) whilst the regulator is open, or (2) whilst the injectors are working. This is done to keep down the concentration of soluble salts in the boiler water to minimise priming.

The valve is fitted on the back plate of the firebox, having a connection above the crown (see Fig. 30).

In the case of (1), steam from the steam chest actuates a piston in the blowdown valve, which in turn lifts a ball valve from its seating, allowing boiler water at the rate of about 1-1½ gallons per minute to be discharged into the ashpan. On some locomotives (2) the

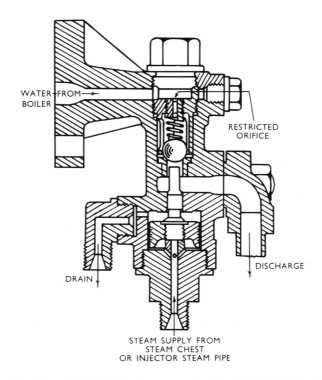

WATER FROM
BOILER

RESTRICTED
ORIFICE

DRAIN

DISCHARGE

STEAM SUPPLY FROM
STEAM CHEST
OR INJECTOR STEAM PIPE

Fig. 30 CONTINUOUS BLOWDOWN VALVE

blowdown valve is operated by the pressure in either injector delivery pipe.

Carriage-warming Valve

This valve controls the pressure in the train-heating pipe.

Cab Fittings

Fig. 31 shows the arrangement of cab fittings on B.R. Standard locomotives.

Questions and Answers

(1) *Q.* What are the principal parts of a locomotive boiler?

A. Boiler barrel; outer and inner firebox; flue tubes; smokebox tubeplate; crown, firebox and longitudinal stays, dome, smokebox, superheater, brick arch, ashpan, firedoor and fusible plugs.

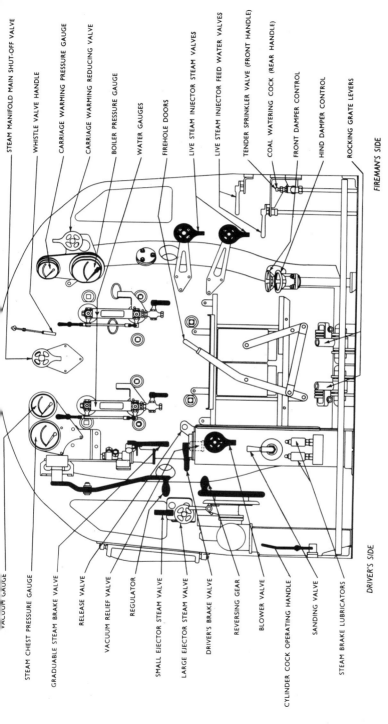

VACUUM GAUGE

STEAM MANIFOLD MAIN SHUT-OFF VALVE

WHISTLE VALVE HANDLE

CARRIAGE WARMING PRESSURE GAUGE

CARRIAGE WARMING REDUCING VALVE

BOILER PRESSURE GAUGE

WATER GAUGES

FIREHOLE DOORS

LIVE STEAM INJECTOR STEAM VALVES

LIVE STEAM INJECTOR FEED WATER VALVES

TENDER SPRINKLER VALVE (FRONT HANDLE)

COAL WATERING COCK (REAR HANDLE)

FRONT DAMPER CONTROL

HIND DAMPER CONTROL

ROCKING GRATE LEVERS

FIREMAN'S SIDE

STEAM CHEST PRESSURE GAUGE

GRADUABLE STEAM BRAKE VALVE

RELEASE VALVE

VACUUM RELIEF VALVE

REGULATOR

SMALL EJECTOR STEAM VALVE

LARGE EJECTOR STEAM VALVE

DRIVER'S BRAKE VALVE

REVERSING GEAR

BLOWER VALVE

CYLINDER COCK OPERATING HANDLE

SANDING VALVE

STEAM BRAKE LUBRICATORS

DRIVER'S SIDE

Fig. 31   ARRANGEMENT OF CAB FITTINGS
Standard Locomotive

Fig. 31

(2) *Q*. What is the function of the safety valves?

A. To prevent the pressure of the steam in the boiler from rising above the registered pressure of the boiler.

(3) *Q*. What is the registered pressure of the boiler?

A. The steam pressure for which the boiler was designed. This is indicated by a metal tablet secured to the firebox back plate and also by a red line on the dial of the steam pressure gauge. If the steam pressure at which the safety valves lift does not correspond within 5 lb. above or below that shown on the pressure gauge as registered pressure, the matter must be reported.

(4) *Q*. Does the escape of steam from the safety valves entail loss?

A. Yes. It represents a waste of labour, coal and water which can largely be avoided by careful management of the fire. It is estimated that for each minute the safety valves are open the wastage of coal is from 10 to 15 lbs. and over 10 gallons of water.

(5) *Q*. Describe the action of the "Pop" safety valve.

A. When the registered pressure is reached the spring-loaded valve rises and admits a small amount of steam through a lip in the valve to the outer annular chamber. This steam escapes through holes in the top cap of the valve (Fig. 16). The steam on escaping acts on the increased area of the top cap and adds to the force which keeps the valve raised till such time as the pressure in the boiler falls, when the valve is instantaneously closed at slightly below the pressure as that at which it opened.

(6) *Q*. Where are the water gauges positioned?

A. The water gauges are mounted on the boiler back plate in the engine cab; the bottom gauge cock is so placed that when the water level is in sight at the bottom of the glass the crown of the firebox is covered with water. When working under normal conditions the level of the water should be kept in sight in the top half of the gauge glass, and before descending severe grades or working over curves with maximum super-elevation of rails, a higher water level should be carried.

(7) *Q*. What are fusible plugs and where are they situated?

A. The fusible plugs are screwed into the firebox crown usually about 1 ft. from the firebox tubeplate and about 1 ft. from the firebox back plate (Fig. 7). These brass plugs have a lead centre or core which melts at a comparatively low temperature. Should the water above the firebox crown fall to a dangerously low level, the plug becomes uncovered and the lead is melted, thus admitting steam and water into the firebox and warning the Enginemen.

(8) *Q.* What action would you take in the event of a melted fusible plug?

A. Put on both injectors to raise the water level in the boiler and take immediate steps to remove or deaden the fire.

(9) *Q.* What are washout plugs, handhole and mudhole doors and for what purpose are they used?

A. Washout plugs, handhole and mudhole doors are removed at washout period for cleaning and examination of the boiler. Washout plugs are fitted on the boiler back plate, smokebox tubeplate, sides of firebox and on throat plate, also on top side of boiler barrel, near the feed trays, on taper boiler engines. Mudhole doors are usually fitted at front and back of the firebox just above the foundation ring and at the side of the firebox opposite each water space. Handhole doors are fitted at side of the firebox above the inside firebox crown.

(10) *Q.* Where is the blower valve and ring positioned and for what purpose is it used?

A. The blower valve is generally situated on the boiler back plate; steam from the dome is led to this valve and when the valve is opened the steam is carried by an internal steam pipe, passing through the boiler, to the smokebox tubeplate, whence it is led to the blower ring or casting on top of the blast pipe or to a blower ring cast integral with the base of the chimney. On B.R. standard locomotives it is mounted below the Driver's brake valve away from the boiler back plate so as to be within easy reach of the driver (see Fig. 21). The function of the blower is to create a partial vacuum in the smokebox when the regulator is closed. Whilst working a train or light engine, the blower valve must always be opened prior to closing the regulator to prevent back draught from the firebox and to avoid smokebox gases being induced down the blast pipe, especially on entering tunnels. Care should always be taken when passing over water troughs to see that the ashpan dampers and firedoor are closed (on the train engine) and the blower valve opened as a further caution to prevent back draught. When the locomotive is standing, the blower may be used to avoid smoke and to augment the natural draught in the firebox when required to raise steam pressure.

(11) *Q.* Describe how the vertical slide valve type of regulator works.

A. The valve is positioned vertically in the dome (Fig. 20); usually the face has four ports, two small ports for starting purposes and two large ports for normal running. Resting on the valve face is the main valve which has four ports cut in it, and the pilot or starting valve rest in turn upon the main valve with a flat spring bearing against it. The pilot valve has usually two ports which are used for starting purposes.

The sequence of movements when operating the regulator is as follows: first movement of the regulator handle lifts the pilot valve until the two small starting ports are open. Further movement of the handle then moves both the pilot valve and the main valve together, which action opens the large ports in the main valve and closes the starting ports. During closing, the pilot valve is first moved down over the main valve to its normal position, and then both valves are brought back to their original position, closing the main ports as they come down.

The independent movement of the pilot valve is obtained by the use of a circular hole for the operating pin in the pilot valve and elongated hole or slot in the main valve, the result being that the latter does not move until the pin has travelled a distance corresponding to the clearance in the slotted hole, a distance which is equal to the lap plus the port of the pilot valve.

(12) *Q*. What purpose is served by the continuous blowdown valve?
  A. To keep down the concentration of soluble salts in the boiler water on regions where water softening is in use, and this is done by allowing a small measured quantity of water to pass out of the boiler continuously whilst (*a*) the regulator is open, or (*b*) whilst injectors are working (Fig. 30). The use of this fitting, therefore, will tend to prevent priming.

(13) *Q*. What is the purpose of the manual-operated blowdown valve?
  A. Whilst the continuous blowdown valve deals with dissolved solids in the water it does not assist with the discharge of the soft sludge which gradually accumulates in the bottom of the boiler barrel and firebox water spaces. To remove this sludge some locomotives are fitted with a manual-operated blowdown valve positioned just above the foundation ring at the centre of the firebox throat plate. This valve is operated by hand lever on the right side of the cab, separate instructions being issued for its use according to the district in which the locomotive may be working.

(14) *Q*. What is priming and foaming? What would you do when either occurs?

A. Priming is produced by certain conditions of the water as well as carrying a too high water level, and may be brought about by a sudden demand for steam which may result in syphoning action or it may be caused by uneven boiling. It is distinct from foaming in that it does not originate at the steaming surface, but at points below the water line. Foaming consists of an aggregation of bubbles which carry the sediment to the surface of the water. In both cases water is carried over with the steam to the cylinders. The more serious effects of priming and foaming in locomotive boilers are the impairment of lubrication due to water and suspended matter passing into the cylinders: interference with the proper functioning of the superheater, due to accumulation of water which must be evaporated before increase of temperature can take place, and in addition the superheater elements may be fouled with solid matter. The water accumulated in the cylinders may also cause damage to the cylinders and motion of the engine.

When priming and foaming occurs with a low water level, open the cylinder cocks, put on the injectors and close the regulator gently until the water settles in the boiler to ascertain the water level, as there is danger of exposing the firebox crown.

(15) *Q*. What is the purpose of feed-water treatment?

A. All natural water contains suspended and dissolved matter, the most common being the acid salts of calcium and magnesium. Treating boiler feed water brings about the precipitation of scale-forming salts which causes the resulting suspended matter to be of such form as to be readily removed as a sludge, thereby keeping the firebox plates and tubes in a much cleaner condition than is the case when untreated water containing scale-forming salts is used.

(16) *Q*. What is the best system for using injectors?

A. Where two live steam injectors are fitted they should always be used in turn to keep both in working order.

(17) *Q*. What depth of water should be maintained in the boiler as a good working level?

A. To maintain the water level in the gauge glass at half to three-quarters full is best. This provides a good depth of water over the firebox and at the same time leaves plenty of steam space.

(18) *Q*. What ill-effects will result from having too much water in the boiler?

A. Too high water level in the boiler is bad practice. It restricts the steam space and leads to water being carried over with the steam, which may cause such troubles as damaged cylinders and pistons, bent connecting rods, possible difficulty in releasing the vacuum brake, and injector troubles.

(19) *Q*. Explain the working principles of a movable combining-cone type of injector.

A. Fig. 25 shows this injector which is usually placed vertically at the inside of the trailing engine footstep. A jet of steam emerging at high velocity from the (top) steam cone is brought into contact with the cold feed water which is admitted round the tip of the steam cone. Partial condensation of the steam jet takes place, a partial vacuum is formed, and the water is forced forward at considerable speed into the wide end of the converging combining cone. Passage through this cone completes the condensation of the steam, producing a high vacuum, and the water emerges from the small end of the cone at greatly increased velocity. The water jet then passes the overflow gap and enters a diverging cone known as the delivery cone.

The shape of the delivery cone causes the speed of the flow to be quickly and considerably reduced, which process converts the energy of motion in the water into pressure energy at the outlet end of the delivery cone. The pressure developed in this way at the delivery end of the injector exceeds the boiler pressure sufficiently to enable the feed water to lift the clack valve against the steam pressure and enter the boiler.

The vacuum developed in the combining cone when the injector is working is used to hold a movable section of the cone up against the top portion, giving the effect of a continuous cone. If the action of the injector is interrupted or the water jet upset, the vacuum in the cone is replaced by pressure, the moving section is then forced away from its seating and any surplus steam and water escapes through the gap so formed, to the overflow outlet. When the pressure has been relieved the working vacuum rapidly re-establishes itself and the injector will then restart. In some types of injectors the moving cone is replaced by a hinged flap forming one side of the combining cone. In this case the flap is forced open when the injector "flies off". Injectors with sliding cone or hinged flap are known as automatic restarting injectors.

(20) *Q.* What is the purpose of the exhaust steam injector?

    A. To provide an economical method of injecting water into the boiler by utilising steam from the blast pipe for this purpose. Exhaust steam also heats the feed water so that a hot feed is obtained. For best results the injector should be at work when the regulator is open, the feed being regulated by the handle provided. The hottest feed is obtained when the feed handle is in the "minimum" position.

(21) *Q.* Name the cones in the exhaust injector.

    A. Supplementary live steam cone, movable exhaust steam cone for regulating water supply (except in the "K" type), draft tube, vacuum tube, combining cone and delivery cone. There is also the auxiliary live steam nozzle, and ports around the supplementary cone.

(22) *Q.* What are the main differences between the "H" and "J" types of exhaust steam injectors?

    A. The two pivoted exhaust steam valves in the "H" type are replaced in the "J" type by a double-beat spring-loaded valve fitted vertically and controlled by a steam piston below the valve. The automatic shuttle valve or change-over valve is fitted below the "J"-type injector with the addition of an automatic choke valve to regulate the quantity of auxiliary steam supplied to the injector when the regulator valve is shut. In the "J" type the automatic water control valve has been replaced by a manual-operated disc water valve on the body of the injector above the water entrance to the nozzles. This disc valve is fitted directly on to and worked by the water regulator spindle and rotated by it. The water valve merely acts as a water-admission valve and does not regulate the quantity of water admitted to the injector cones, which is controlled by the movable exhaust steam cone as in the "H"-type injector. To shut off the "J"-type injector the steam valve is closed and the water regulator spindle moved to the shut position.

(23) *Q.* What is the "H/J" exhaust steam injector?

    A. This is an exhaust injector of the "H" type retaining the automatic water control valve but embracing the front or live and exhaust steam portion of the "J" type, i.e. the casting containing the exhaust steam control, change-over control system and automatic choke valve. The main body of the injector, containing the cones, automatic water valve and details of the "H" type, is retained.

(24) *Q.* How would you test the automatic change-over in the exhaust steam injector?

A. To test the automatic change-over from live steam to exhaust steam and vice versa apply engine brake with engine standing, start injector working and then open engine regulator. If the automatic shuttle valve functions properly the injector will stop working and water will run out of overflow. Then close the regulator and open the cylinder cocks. When pressure has escaped from the engine cylinders the injector will immediately work. If the injector does not operate as described and continues to work with the regulator open, the automatic shuttle valve does not function. Either a restriction will be found in the auxiliary steam pipe from the steam chest to the injector or the automatic check valve does not seat properly.

(25) *Q.* If the auxiliary control pipe from the steam chest breaks while running, what should be done?

A. If possible, carry on to first stopping point then blank off the pipe at a union or close isolating cock where fitted; if unable to do this, flatten the pipe on the steam chest side of the fracture. The injector will still work on live steam with this pipe blanked off. If the exhaust steam pipe, from the blast pipe to the injector, fractures whilst running, the auxiliary control pipe from the steam chest would have to be blanked off to allow the injector to operate with live steam while regulator valve was open, although injector would work normally with regulator closed.

(26) *Q.* If one of the top feed clacks sticks up when working a train, what steps would you take?

A. Immediately put on the opposite injector and then note whether the boiler will supply the demand for steam required to work the train in addition to the loss from the sticking clack. If it will not, the train should be stopped at next point where it can be placed under protection of fixed signals, where steps should be taken to re-seat the clack. To do this, close the tank or tender feed valve and the blow-back steam will exhaust at the injector overflow; open the water regulator valve wide; open the injector steam valve fully to expel the blow-back steam and to create a partial vacuum in the injector body; open the tank feed quickly and the injector should pick up the water and, when regulated, the delivery will disturb the clack which should re-seat when the injector is shut off.

(27) *Q.* If your engine is giving trouble with leaking tubes or stays, what is the best procedure to adopt?

A. In this case the Driver should do all in his power to ease the demand on the boiler and assist the Fireman by working the engine as lightly as possible. It is better to lose a few minutes in running than to come to a forced stop in a section, thereby causing heavy delays by having to carry out Protection Rules. The Fireman should exercise the greatest care in manipulation of the injector, dampers and firedoor, in order to maintain the firebox temperature as steady as possible.

(28) *Q.* Name several preventable causes of engines not steaming.

A. Dirty firebox tubeplate, tubes blocked up, leaking joints in smokebox, tubes leaking, blast pipe out of alignment with chimney, smokebox door drawing air (not properly tightened up), defective brick arch, defective dampers, valves and pistons blowing through, inefficient firing, badly fitting baffle plate and choked ash plate (spark arrester) in smokebox of the self-cleaning type.

SECTION 5

VALVES AND PISTONS

The steam locomotive is the means of converting the heat energy contained in the fuel into useful work by driving the pistons, the reciprocating motion of these being converted into the rotary motion of the driving wheels by the piston rod, connecting rod and cranks.

When the regulator valve is opened, steam generated in the boiler passes through the internal steam pipe (and superheater when fitted), through the external steam pipe to the steam chest, where the supply of steam to the cylinders is regulated by the action of the valves, In the cylinders the steam expands and does useful work on the piston before escaping into the atmosphere.

The locomotive valve of any kind must, in conjunction with the valve gear, so control the valve that the following events take place in succession in the cylinder:—

(*a*) A period of admission of live steam up to a point of cut-off.

(*b*) A period of expansion up to a point of release.

(*c*) A period of release for the used steam.

(*d*) A period of compression after the valve has closed.

(*e*) A brief period of pre-admission of live steam before the piston commences its working stroke (see Fig. 32).

In the events just indicated the valve has three distinct duties to perform:—

(*a*) closes both steam ports when in its central position;

(*b*) admits steam to one end of the cylinder only at one time;

(*c*) opens to exhaust at one end of the cylinder at least as soon as it opens to admit steam at the other.

Figs. 33 and 33A show sections through steam chests in which slide and piston valves operate. The face on which the valve slides has three ports, the end ports "A" lead one to each end of the cylinder, the larger centre port "C" leads to the exhaust passage. In the position shown in the bottom figure, steam from the steam chest is passing the edge of the valve into the left-hand steam port, exerting a pressure, driving the piston to the right. On the other side of the piston steam is escaping by way of the right-hand steam port, through the cavity in the slide valve to the exhaust passage.

The relative positions of the valve and piston (ordinary "D" slide valve and inside admission piston valve) for one revolution of the wheel are shown in Fig. 34.

It will be noted that the slide or piston valve controlling the

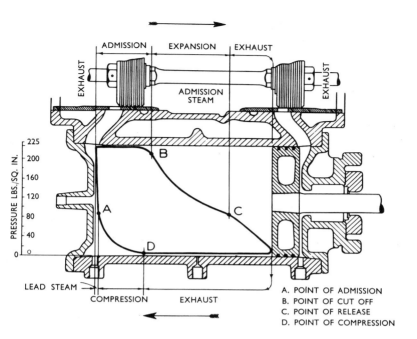

A. POINT OF ADMISSION
B. POINT OF CUT OFF
C. POINT OF RELEASE
D. POINT OF COMPRESSION

Fig. 32 DIAGRAM SHOWING THE DISTRIBUTION OF STEAM ON ONE SIDE OF THE PISTON FOR A DOUBLE STROKE

admission and exhaustion of steam to and from the cylinders has its face of such breadth that when the valve is in mid position it completely closes both steam ports. Two more important items have to be considered now—the "lap" and "lead" of the valve. "Lap" is the amount by which the valve overlaps each steam port at the middle position of each valve. There are actually two kinds of lap: "steam lap" is the amount by which the valve overlaps the port on the live steam side; similarly, the "exhaust lap" is the amount by which the valve overlaps the port on the exhaust side. "Exhaust lap" is generally given to slow-running locomotives, i.e. those designed for shunting duties, the effect being to delay the exhaust and derive the maximum work from the expanding steam in the cylinder.

"Negative exhaust lap", or as commonly termed "exhaust clearance" (Fig. 33), is the amount the port is open to exhaust when

Fig. 33 SECTION SLIDE AND PISTON VALVE

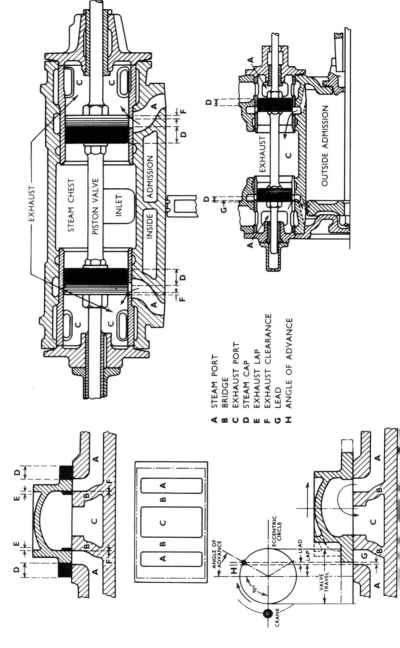

A STEAM PORT
B BRIDGE
C EXHAUST PORT
D STEAM CAP
E EXHAUST LAP
F EXHAUST CLEARANCE
G LEAD
H ANGLE OF ADVANCE

Fig. 33

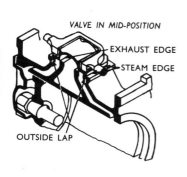

VALVE IN MID-POSITION

EXHAUST EDGE

STEAM EDGE

OUTSIDE LAP

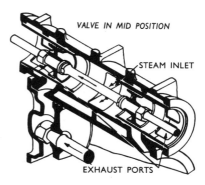

VALVE IN MID POSITION

STEAM INLET

EXHAUST PORTS

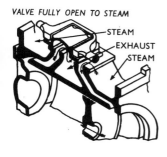

VALVE FULLY OPEN TO STEAM

STEAM

EXHAUST

STEAM

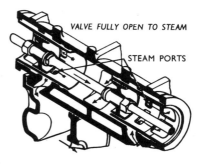

VALVE FULLY OPEN TO STEAM

STEAM PORTS

**SLIDE VALVE
AND STEAM CHEST**

**PISTON VALVE
AND STEAM CHEST**

Fig. 33a

the valve is in mid-position, and this is used on many fast-running locomotives to give a free exhaust. The amount seldom exceeds $\frac{1}{16}$ in. when exhaust clearance is given; the cylinder on both sides of the piston is open to exhaust at the same time when the valve is passing through the mid-position, which is only momentary when running.

The "lead" of the valve is the amount by which the steam port is open when the piston is static at front or back dead centre. Pre-admission of steam fills the clearance space between the cylinder and piston and ensures maximum cylinder pressure at the commencement of the stroke. "Lead" is particularly necessary on locomotives designed for high speeds, under which conditions the valve events are taking place in rapid succession.

84

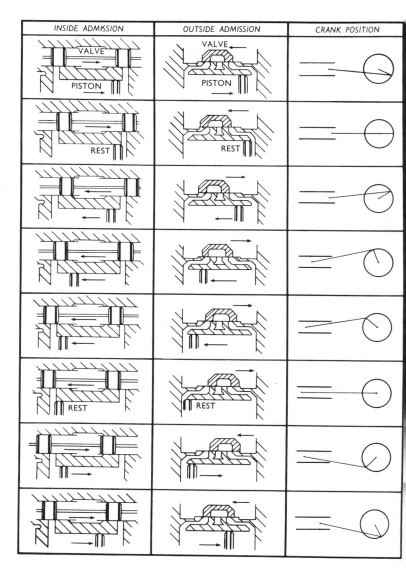

**Fig. 34 VALVE EVENTS
FOR ONE REVOLUTION OF WHEEL**

Fig. 35 ECCENTRIC CRANK AND RETURN CRANK

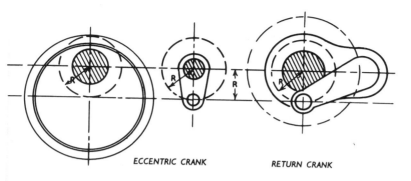

ECCENTRIC CRANK   RETURN CRANK

The eccentric (Fig. 35) is used to convert the rotary motion of the crank axle into the reciprocating motion required to operate the valve. If we imagine a "D"-type slide valve without "lap" and not given "lead" it would, when the piston is at the end of its stroke, just cover the steam ports and be in the central position, i.e. mid-stroke. The eccentric operating the valve would also be in mid-position and set at 90° (a right-angle) in advance of the crank. From this position the valve would commence to open.

The eccentric is equivalent to a small crank, the length of whose arm "R" is the same as the distance between the centre of the eccentric sheave and centre of shaft. The length of "R" is called the eccentricity of the eccentric, and the valve travel is equal to twice the eccentricity. The return crank gives an equivalent movement to that of the eccentric and describes a circle of radius equal to distance "R" between the centre of the shaft or axle and the centre of the return crank pin.

If "steam lap" is added to the valve it would overlap the port by the amount of "lap" and if the eccentric were set as described above, steam would not be admitted to the cylinder until the piston had travelled some distance from dead centre and the engine would not work properly. To overcome this difficulty and to admit steam through the steam port to behind the piston immediately it moves from dead centre, the valve must be set ahead of the crank by 90° plus the "steam lap" (see Fig. 33). It is necessary also, as we have previously stated, to provide "lead" and this is done by moving the eccentric still further in advance of the crank; the eccentric has therefore been moved through a total of 90° plus "lap", plus "lead", the angle in excess of the right-angle being known as the "angle of advance".

It should be remembered that only the "lap" is apparent on the valve, the "lead" being a portion of the port opening, but both the "lap" and "lead" are apparent on the setting of the eccentric.

From mid-position the travel of the valve is equal to the "lap" plus the steam port opening, this being equal to the throw of the eccentric or the radius of eccentricity (see Fig. 35).

Twice the throw of the eccentric will be equal to the full travel of the valve, just as twice the throw of the main crank equals the stroke of the piston. Whilst the "lead" affects the angular advance of the eccentric it does not affect the travel of the valve.

The piston valve (Figs. 33 and 33a) consists of two circular pistons fixed the necessary distance apart on a spindle; the whole assembly reciprocates in a cylindrical steam chest. The valve heads are each fitted with rings to maintain a steam-tight fit in the steam chest. Piston valves can be adapted for inside or outside admission of steam to the cylinders. With inside-admission piston valves the live steam is contained between the two heads and is admitted to the steam ports at the inner edges of the valve heads, being exhausted at the outer edges into separate exhaust passages which combine to communicate with the blast pipe.

With outside-admission piston valves the steam is contained outside the valve heads with a common exhaust chamber between the heads, steam entering the ports at the outer edges of the valve heads and being exhausted at the inner edges.

With this arrangement the valve spindle glands are subjected to high-pressure steam at high temperature in the case of superheated locomotives and for this reason modern locomotives are almost invariably of the inside-admission type. Exceptions are the former S.R. Merchant Navy and West Country classes which have outside-admission valves, but which employ steam chest rocking shafts in place of valve spindle glands, as shown in Fig. 50. The modified former S.R. "Pacific's" have normal Walschaert valve gear, but whilst the inside cylinder has inside admission the outside ones have outside admission.

With inside-admission piston valves the travel of the valve is opposite that of the slide valve and outside steam admission piston valve; thus, to admit steam to the front port the valve must be moved forward to allow steam to pass the inside edge of the front valve head, i.e. in a direction opposite to that of the cylinder piston. The setting of the eccentrics in each case is shown in Fig. 35A.

When using a direct-acting link motion with inside-admission piston valves the eccentric requires to be set an additional 180° in advance of the crank to that used for outside admission, which position is actually following the crank by 90° minus "lead".

Inside-admission piston valves actuated by means of a rocking shaft, which reverses the direction of travel of the valve motion, require the eccentrics to be set as with direct motion with slide valves.

The maximum travel of the slide or piston valve is twice the "steam lap" plus twice the port openings. The minimum travel is twice the "lap" plus twice the mid-gear "lead".

The chief points affecting steam flows are valve travel, the diameter of the piston valves, together with the shape and layout of the steam chest and port passages.

The width of the steam ports in the valve liner is dependent upon the travel: the longer the travel, the wider the ports can be made. The extension of the steam chest beyond the ends of the cylinder barrel enables the piston valve heads to be widely spaced so that the

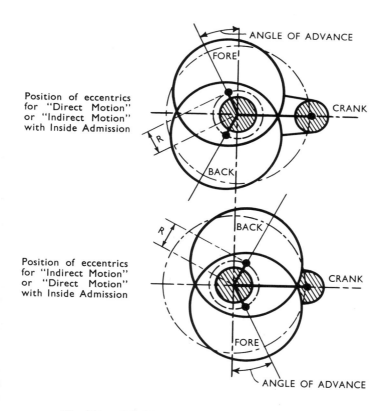

Fig. 35a POSITION OF ECCENTRICS

steam ports can be located directly at the ends of the cylinder bore, allowing direct passages between the valve ports and the cylinder.

The term "long travel" is actually a "long lap" valve, the increased steam lap being greater in proportion than the increase in valve travel. The chief advantage derived from long-lap valves is greater exhaust freedom and earlier cut-off working, the valve moving a greater distance for a given angular movement of the crank. The initial movement of the valve is accelerated, being the valve events of admission, expansion, exhaustion and compression more sharply defined. The port opening to steam is increased and both the exhaust and compression delayed, at the same time the greater port opening to exhaust provides a free exhaust at high speed and a decrease in back pressure.

The slide valve has an advantage over the piston valve in that it will lift off the port face to release water which may have accumulated in the cylinders when standing, and although pressure relief valves are fitted to the cylinders of locomotives fitted with piston valves, they are not designed to deal with large quantities of water.

Locomotive pistons are of various types. There are, for instance, the "box" type which is manufactured of cast iron and the "dish" type which is made of cast iron or steel. On former L.N.E.R. standard locomotives, the piston and rod are in one piece, being made of steel forged or welded.

Modern pistons are fitted with two or three narrow rings about $\frac{5}{16}$ in. in width. A B.R. standard design of piston head is shown in Fig. 36.

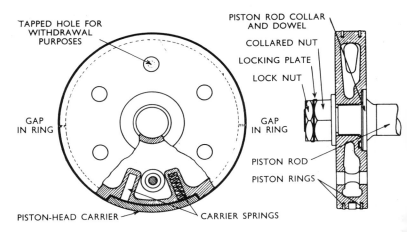

Fig. 36 PISTON HEAD

Cylinder drain cocks are fitted to drain away any accumulation of water from the cylinders and steam chest. Three drain cocks are fitted to each cylinder casting, one at each end of the cylinders and one connected to the steam chest. Cylinder cocks should always be open when the locomotive is standing or at any time when there is an indication of water in the cylinders. Steam-operated cylinder cocks are fitted to some of the B.R. standard locomotives (see Fig. 37).

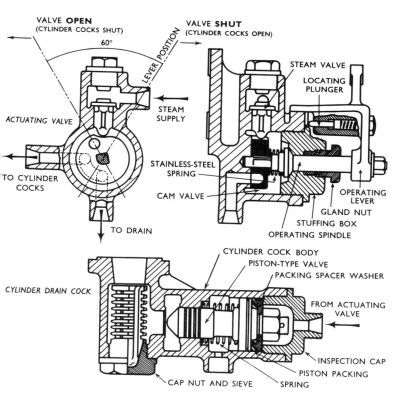

Fig. 37 STEAM-OPERATED ACTUATING VALVE AND CYLINDER DRAIN COCK

Most locomotives with piston valves are fitted with one or more anti-vacuum valves which automatically admit air to minimise the partial vacuum created in the cylinders and steam chests when coasting with the regulator closed. Under these conditions the valves and pistons in the cylinders act like pumps, tending to induce air from the steam chest, which action rapidly creates a partial vacuum inside the steam chest, the amount being further increased by the cylinders during what would be the normal "expansion" portion of the stroke, with the result that when the valve opens to exhaust, smokebox gases and possibly ashes may be drawn down the blast pipe to destroy the vacuum. Additionally, during the compression portion of the stroke very high temperatures are reached which cause lubrication difficulties. To counteract these effects anti-vacuum valves are fitted. These may be placed either on the steam chest or be connected to the saturated side of the superheater header and their effect is to admit air and partially destroy the vacuum in the steam chest (see Figs. 38 and 39). It will be appreciated that these valves are more effective at slow speeds and long cut-offs, i.e. when the expansion and compression periods of the stroke are the shortest. It is not satisfactory, however, to run at high speeds with the valve gear in full travel, nor would the anti-vacuum valves admit sufficient air to be effective. When coasting under these circumstances a breath of steam should be supplied to the steam chest by cracking the regulator, i.e. slightly opening and placing the reversing gear in the best position for the type of locomotive. For locomotives fitted with poppet valves there are special instructions.

Questions and Answers

(1) *Q.* How is the drive conveyed from the pistons to the wheels?

 A. The drive from the piston is conveyed to the wheels by way of the piston rod, crosshead, little end, connecting rod, big end and the crank. The connecting rod and crank convert the backward and forward movement of the piston into the rotary movement of the axle and wheel.

 In forward gear the pistons push the crank pins under the axle and pull them forward over it, while in back gear the crank pins are pushed over the axle and pulled forward under it.

 The slide bars or guides prevent the oblique thrust of the connecting rod from bending the piston rod. For example, if the crank is on the top quarter and the piston being propelled forward as in fore gear, the resistance of the crank causes an upward thrust in the connecting rod which is transmitted to the slide bars. The thrust of the piston rod crosshead being against the top slide bar when running forwards and against the bottom bar when running backwards, with regulator open.

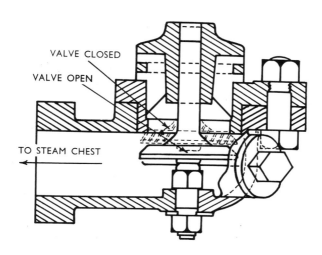

**Fig. 38 ANTI-VACUUM VALVE
MOUNTED ON STEAM CHEST**

VALVE CLOSED

VALVE OPEN

TO STEAM CHEST

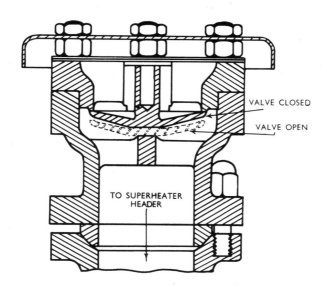

**Fig. 39 ANTI-VACUUM VALVE
MOUNTED ON SUPERHEATER HEADER**

VALVE CLOSED

VALVE OPEN

TO SUPERHEATER
HEADER

When the crank pin drives the piston, as when coasting, the direction of the thrust on the slide bar is reversed. The amount of thrust varies with the angularity of the connecting rod, being greatest at about half stroke when the crank and connecting rod are at right-angles to each other, being reduced to zero at the dead centre, hence the increased wear in the middle of the slide bars.

(2) *Q*. What are the eight named positions of the crank?

A. The forward and backward crank position in which the crank pin, connecting rod and piston are all in a straight line are known as the front and back dead centres. When the crank pin stands at right-angles to the centre line, upwards or downwards, it is said to be on the top or bottom quarter. The four intermediate settings which lie mid-way between the front and back dead centres and the top and bottom quarters are known respectively as the front and back top angles and the front and back bottom angles (see Fig. 40).

(3) *Q*. Does the position of the crank supply any clue to the position of the piston in the cylinder?

A. Yes. By reference to the eight crank positions described in the previous question it is quite easy to visualise the position of the piston within the cylinder. For instance, when the crank is on front or back dead centre the piston will be at the end of its stroke at the front or back of the cylinder, when the crank is on the top or bottom quarter the piston will be approximately at mid-stroke. With the crank on top or bottom front angle the piston will be rather less than quarter stroke from the front of the cylinder and rather less than quarter stroke from the back cover when the crank is on either of the two angles.

(4) *Q*. What is the relation between the events in the steam cycle and piston position?

A. The duration of the various periods of steam in the cylinder is generally measured in terms of the piston stroke, for instance, when we refer to cut-off at 50% or 75%. It is, therefore, possible to state where the piston will be when the events of cut-off, release, compression and admission occur. Consequently it is only one step further from this to be able to couple the cylinder events with the crank settings to enable the valve position to be judged from the setting of the cranks or side rods.

(5) *Q*. The steam action in the cylinder has been explained in relation to the piston movement. Can you explain it in relation to the crank positions?

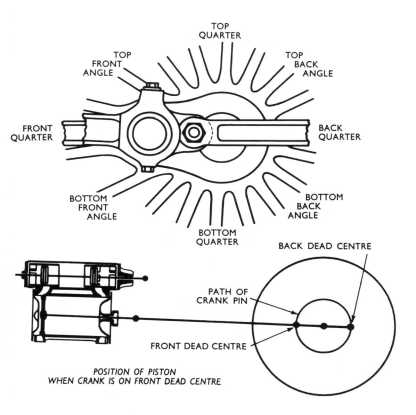

Fig. 40   LEAST-EFFORT POSITION OF CRANK

A. In forward gear the front side of the piston is exposed to live steam during admission and expansion periods and the rear side is exhausting as the crank moves under the axle from front dead centre to back dead centre. After the crank passes back dead centre position the back of the piston takes admission steam followed by expansion and the front side of the piston enters upon the exhaust and compression periods.

In back gear steam acts in front of the piston as the crank passes over the axle and behind the piston as the crank moves forward under the axle.

(6) *Q*. What is the effect of notching up the gear upon the steam cycle with the cylinder?

A. Notching up shortens the valve travel, this having the effect of shortening the admission period and lengthening the expansion and compression periods.

(7) *Q*. When the crank is on top or bottom position the piston would be approximately at mid-stroke. Why do these positions of the crank not place the piston exactly at mid-stroke?

A. This effect is produced by the angularity, the piston will occupy the exact centre of the cylinder barrel only in the crank positions where the angle between the centre line of the crank pins and the centre line on the connecting rod is equal to 90°, this will occur when the crank pin is slightly in advance of the top and bottom quarter positions.

The extent of this angularity effect depends upon the length of the connecting rod and the throw of the crank and is increased when short connecting rods are used. Allowance has to be made for this effect in the valve gear, otherwise steam distribution would be adversely affected.

(8) *Q*. Describe in detail a typical steam cycle in the front end of the cylinder during one revolution of the driving wheels, the gear being in a position giving about 30% cut-off.

A. Commencing from the dead centre the piston will travel about 30% of its stroke before the valve closes the front port to steam and cut-off occurs. Expansion will occupy a further 45% of the stroke, at which point the exhaust edge of the valve will uncover the front port to exhaust giving the point of release, the piston then completes the remaining 25% of the backward stroke with the front port open to exhaust. The piston will now make about 70% of the return stroke before the exhaust edge of the valve again closes the front port starting the period of compression. This will occupy about 25% of the return stroke, at which point the steam edge of the valve clears the front port, once more opening it to lead. This is the period of pre-admission which occupies the remaining 5% of the return stroke until the piston reaches the front dead-centre position in readiness for the commencement of the next cycle (see Fig. 32).

(9) *Q*. What is occurring in the back of the cylinder during the same period?

A. Starting from the front dead centre the valve already has the back port open to exhaust, which continues until the piston has covered 70% of the backward stroke, when the valve closes the back port and compression commences. This occupies a further 25% of the stroke, when the steam edge of the valve will uncover the back port to lead and the period of pre-admission sets in to occupy the remaining 5% of the backward stroke. The piston now returns from the back dead centre and will cover about 30% of the return stroke before cut-off occurs at the back port. Expansion then follows for another 45% of the stroke, after which the back port is again opened to exhaust and release occurs, lasting over the remaining 25% of the stroke until the piston reaches front dead centre.

(10) *Q.* How can you tell which crank leads?

A. The engine should be set with one big end on the top quarter and if the other big end is then on the front dead centre the latter crank leads, if on the back dead centre it follows.

(11) *Q.* How should a locomotive be set in order to test the valves and pistons on one side? Describe the procedure.

A. The crank of the cylinder under test should be set on the top or bottom quarter, the reversing lever placed in mid-gear and the regulator opened slightly with the steam and hand brake on and the cylinder cocks closed.

The test is made by moving the reversing lever as required from forward to backward gear and noting the indications given at chimney or cylinder cocks.

If on going into full forward gear a blow is heard from the chimney which ceases in mid-gear and restarts in back gear, leakage past the piston will be indicated.

A continuous blow up the chimney obtained in all positions of the reversing lever would indicate that the valve under test was blowing through, but on two-cylinder locomotives this effect would also be produced by a defective piston on the opposite side, and therefore if this indication is obtained, reset the engine and test the other cylinder in order to prove the opposite piston before coming to any decision.

(12) *Q.* What indication would be given by this test if the valves and pistons were in good order?

A. In this case no blow will be heard from the chimney in any position of the gear, but a single and well-defined beat will be heard as the gear is reversed from forward to back gear and vice versa.

(13) *Q.* How would you test for a broken valve lap on a slide valve engine or admission steam rings on a piston valve engine?

A. This may be found with big end on bottom quarter setting as described above, but the cylinder cocks should be left open.

If on moving the reversing gear a short distance towards forward gear steam blows from the front cock, or from the back cock when the reversing gear is moved a short distance toward back gear, this indicates that a portion is broken off the front or back valve lap respectively. In the case of a piston valve a broken ring or damaged steam edge of the valve would be indicated. In the case of badly damaged laps, a blow from either of the cocks may be obtained with the lever in mid-gear according to which lap is affected. The front laps may also be tested with cranks set on the front angles and the back laps with cranks set on the back angles if desired.

(14) *Q*. Describe the principle of the angles tests using front angles setting.

A. In this position two crossheads will be level in the slide bars next to the front end, and with the reversing gear in mid-position both front ports will be just covered by the steam edges of the valves, whilst the two back ports will be open to exhaust. In forward gear the R.H. valve will uncover the front port to steam and will maintain the back port to exhaust. The L.H. valve will open the front port to exhaust and will close the back port. In backward gear the R.H. valve opens the front port to steam and the back port to exhaust.

(15) *Q*. If your engine was suspected of having a cracked valve cavity or defective piston valve rings, causing a bad blow through to exhaust, could you ascertain which valve was at fault?

A. Yes. This could be ascertained by employing the mid-stroke tests with crank on top or bottom quarter, but it would be advisable to test both sides. In this test the cylinder cocks should be used and when the defective side is tested steam will be found to issue from both front and back cylinder cocks when the gear is in forward and backward gear. In forward gear a heavy blow will be obtained from the front cock and a light blow from the back, whilst in back gear the back cock will blow heavily and the front one lightly. On former G.W.R. locomotives fitted with piston valves the test required is slightly different as the valves are fitted with only two rings on each head, i.e. one steam and one exhaust. In this case the suspected side should be placed with big end on the bottom, cylinder cocks open, brake hard on, reversing lever in mid-gear. With the regulator open, steam from the front cylinder cock indicates that the front steam ring is defective. No steam from either cylinder cock indicates that steam rings on both heads are good.

Close cylinder cocks and put reversing lever into full forward gear, open regulator to fill front end of cylinder with steam and then shut. Bring back reversing gear nearly to mid-gear and retain in this position for a few seconds. In this position the exhaust ring is on the exhaust side of the port, thus keeping the steam in the cylinder. If steam is blowing through to exhaust in this position no beat will be heard up the chimney when the reversing lever is moved into back gear; the front exhaust ring is defective. If, however, a good beat is heard when the reversing lever is placed into back gear the front exhausting ring is good. By placing the lever into back gear and then following the same procedure the back exhaust ring may be tested.

Note: A blow up the chimney in both fore and back gear would indicate a defective piston.

(16) *Q.* How can the valves and pistons be tested on a three-cylinder simple engine?

A. Each cylinder should be tested separately by the mid-stroke method with crank on top or bottom quarter. Another method is to test each piston separately with its crank on front or back dead centre. By this method a defective piston will be disclosed by a continuous blow up the chimney in all positions of the lever when the regulator is opened, because one port will be open to lead and the other to exhaust. If the piston is sound there will, of course, be no blow of any kind. Whichever method is used, all three pistons must be tested in turn and the results noted before any decision is formed as to where the defect lies, because it is possible to be misled from a single test if defects exist in one or both of the other two cylinders.

(17) *Q.* How can a four-cylinder simple engine be tested for valves and pistons?

A. In this case also the mid-stroke setting should be used, but it has to be realised that the adjacent inside and outside cylinder will be tested simultaneously due to the fact that their respective cranks are fixed on opposite centres.

SECTION 6

VALVE GEARS

We have seen from the previous section that a slide or piston valve actuated by one eccentric will rotate the driving wheels in one direction, but, as it is essential that the engine must work in both directions, additional valve gear becomes necessary.

Two-cylinder locomotives are constructed with the cranks set at right-angles to each other, one piston exerting its greatest effort whilst the other, on its dead centre, will not exert any rotating force on its crank. The piston on the front or back dead centre must receive steam at the end of the cylinder and travel away from the cylinder cover irrespective of whether the engine moves forward or backward. The other piston at mid-stroke will receive steam either at the front or back and will move in the direction of the force exerted, which will determine whether the engine moves forward or backward. The function of the slide or piston valve is to distribute the steam to the cylinder and that of the valve gear to control the valve events in correct sequence.

The Stephenson Valve Gear

This type of valve motion, as shown in Fig. 41, employs two eccentrics, fitted to the crank axle, for each valve, one eccentric for fore- and one for back-gear working.

The backward and forward movement of the eccentrics is transmitted through the eccentric rods to a slotted link known as the expansion link, the fore-gear eccentric rod being coupled to the top and the back-gear rod to the bottom of the link. The links are suspended from a common reversing shaft by lifting links and may be raised or lowered at will from the reversing gear in the cab through the medium of the reversing rod.

Fitted in the slot of the expansion link is a die block, which is connected to the valve spindle by an intermediate valve rod. When the link is lowered to bring the fore-gear eccentric rod into line or almost in line with the intermediate valve rod or spindle rod, the movement of the eccentric is transferred to the valve. Conversely, if the link be raised, the movement of the back-gear eccentric rod will be transferred to the valve. With the link placed so that the die block is in the centre of the link, the mid-gear position, the link simply oscillates about the die block with a to and fro movement equal to the steam lap plus the lead of the valve, from its central

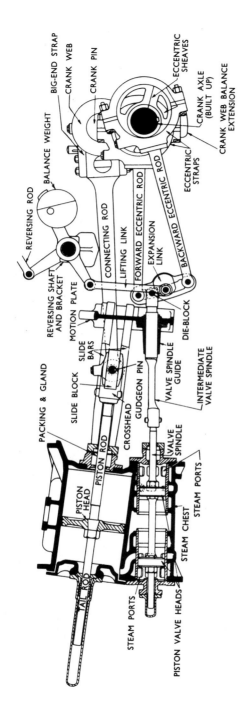

**Fig. 41 STEPHENSON VALVE GEAR
WITH OUTSIDE ADMISSION PISTON VALVES DIRECT MOTION**

BIG-END STRAP
CRANK WEB
CRANK PIN
ECCENTRIC SHEAVES
CRANK AXLE (BUILT UP)
CRANK WEB BALANCE EXTENSION
BALANCE WEIGHT
ECCENTRIC STRAPS
REVERSING ROD
CONNECTING ROD
LIFTING LINK
FORWARD ECCENTRIC ROD
EXPANSION LINK
BACKWARD ECCENTRIC ROD
REVERSING SHAFT AND BRACKET
MOTION PLATE
DIE-BLOCK
SLIDE BARS
VALVE SPINDLE GUIDE
INTERMEDIATE VALVE SPINDLE
PACKING & GLAND
SLIDE BLOCK
CROSSHEAD
GUDGEON PIN
VALVE SPINDLE
PISTON ROD
VALVE SPINDLE
PISTON HEAD
STEAM CHEST
STEAM PORTS
TAIL ROD
STEAM PORTS
PISTON VALVE HEADS
STEAM PORTS

Fig. 41

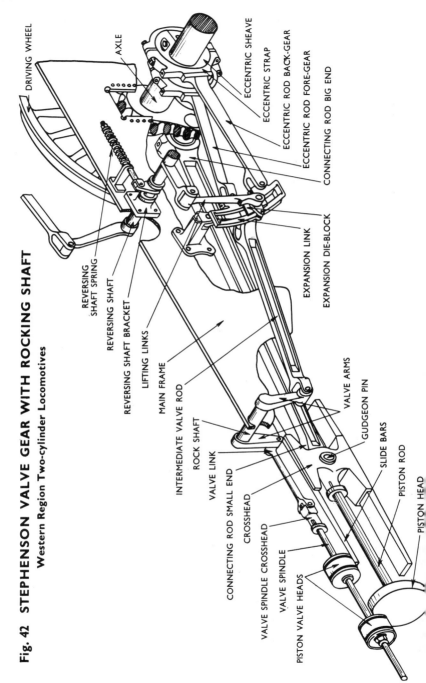

Fig. 42 STEPHENSON VALVE GEAR WITH ROCKING SHAFT
Western Region Two-cylinder Locomotives

DRIVING WHEEL

AXLE

ECCENTRIC SHEAVE

ECCENTRIC STRAP

ECCENTRIC ROD BACK-GEAR

ECCENTRIC ROD FORE-GEAR

CONNECTING ROD BIG END

REVERSING SHAFT SPRING

REVERSING SHAFT

REVERSING SHAFT BRACKET

LIFTING LINKS

MAIN FRAME

EXPANSION LINK

EXPANSION DIE-BLOCK

INTERMEDIATE VALVE ROD

ROCK SHAFT

VALVE LINK

CONNECTING ROD SMALL END

CROSSHEAD

VALVE SPINDLE CROSSHEAD

VALVE SPINDLE

PISTON VALVE HEADS

VALVE ARMS

GUDGEON PIN

SLIDE BARS

PISTON ROD

PISTON HEAD

Fig. 42

Fig. 43 STEPHENSON VALVE GEAR
DIAGRAM SHOWING VARIATION IN LEAD

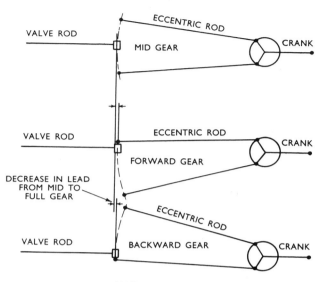

DIAGRAM OF VALVE LEAD

In Stephenson's Gear with Rods as shown in the sketch the valve head gradually increases as the gear is notched up from Full Backward or Full Forward to Midgear and becomes a *Maximum* in Midgear. This is owing to the control of the valve by the eccentrics having a varying effect from Midgear to Full Forward or Backward Gear. At Midgear both eccentrics exercise effect on the movement of the valves giving *Maximum Lead*. When Full Forward or Full Backward Gear is approached one eccentric exercises a decreasing control and the other eccentric an increasing control until Full Gear is reached. The forward eccentric has Full Control in Forward Gear and the backward eccentric Full Control in Back Gear giving *Minimum Lead*.

position. The full travel in mid-gear position is equal to twice the steam lap plus twice the mid-gear lead.

Intermediate positions of the die block in the link will allow for a variation of valve travel, according to the position of the reversing gear, varying the cut-off of steam to the cylinders and making use of the expansive property of the steam.

With the arrangement of the Stephenson link motion, as shown in Figs. 41 and 42, the lead of the valve increases as the gear is "notched up" to a maximum at mid-gear and a minimum at full forward or full backward gear. Fig. 43 illustrates the variation of lead for mid- and full-gear positions; the increase of lead at early cut-off positions is advantageous at high speeds.

Fig. 44 WALSCHAERT VALVE GEAR

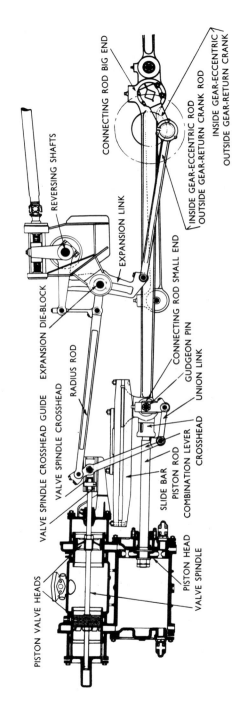

CONNECTING ROD BIG END

INSIDE GEAR-ECCENTRIC ROD
OUTSIDE GEAR-RETURN CRANK ROD

INSIDE GEAR-ECCENTRIC
OUTSIDE GEAR-RETURN CRANK

REVERSING SHAFTS

EXPANSION LINK

EXPANSION DIE-BLOCK

VALVE SPINDLE CROSSHEAD GUIDE

VALVE SPINDLE CROSSHEAD

RADIUS ROD

CONNECTING ROD SMALL END

GUDGEON PIN

UNION LINK

SLIDE BAR

PISTON ROD

COMBINATION LEVER

CROSSHEAD

PISTON VALVE HEADS

PISTON HEAD

VALVE SPINDLE

Fig. 44

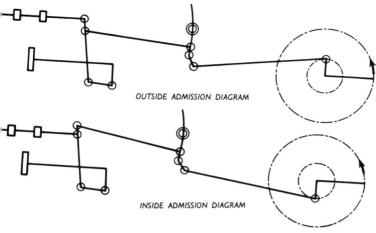

OUTSIDE ADMISSION DIAGRAM

INSIDE ADMISSION DIAGRAM

Fig. 45 ARRANGEMENT FOR WALSCHAERT VALVE GEAR

With outside-admission valves (slide and piston) actuated directly by Stephenson valve gear, the position of the eccentric on the crank axle is 90° plus the angle of advance in front of the crank for each direction of travel.

With inside-admission valves operated directly, the respective eccentrics follow the crank by 90° less the angle of advance.

If a rocking shaft, which reverses the direction of movement, is interposed between the inside-admission valve and the valve gear, the eccentrics are set as mentioned in the first example.

The Walschaert's Valve Gear

With this type of valve gear the movement is derived from two distinct sources, as follows:—

(a) A single eccentric or return crank, eccentric rod or return crank rod, expansion link and radius rod (Fig. 44) which provides for the movement of the valve equal to twice the steam port opening, the expansion link being provided for varying the cut-off and reversing the direction of travel.

(b) A combination lever attached at its lower end to a union link which is connected to the piston crosshead, the upper end of the combination lever being coupled to both the valve spindle and the radius rod, the latter being attached above or below the valve rod, depending upon the use of inside or outside admission valves respectively. The layout of the gear for both types of valves is shown in Fig. 45. Variations of this gear to operate outside cylinders with the valve gear inside as on former G.W.R. locomotives, also outside valve to operate inside cylinders as on the later builds of former L.M.S.R. 4-6-2 are shown in Figs. 46 and 47. Another variation is that used on former L.N.E.R. 3-cylinder locomotives in which the Walschaert valve gear for the outside cylinders operate the inside cylinders through a system of levers (see Fig. 48).

The point at which the radius rod is attached to the combination lever becomes the fulcrum of the whole motion, and the relative movement of the two ends of the lever must be such that the full movement of the crosshead imparted to the lower end of the combination lever will give a movement to the valve spindle equivalent to twice the steam lap plus twice the lead (Fig. 49).

This valve gear is readily adapted to operate with outside or inside cylinders and with slide valves and outside or inside admission piston valves.

The arrangement of the eccentric or return crank to provide movement to the valve beyond that already provided by the combination lever for lap and lead steam depends on whether inside or outside admission valves are employed.

With inside-admission piston valves the eccentric or return crank is set at 90° behind the crank. With outside-admission valves the eccentric or return crank is set at 90° in front of the crank.

The expansion link, suspended at its centre by trunnions, is oscillated an equal amount forward and backward by the eccentric or return crank through the medium of the eccentric rod or return crank rod. An expansion die block slides in the expansion link and is attached to a radius rod which, attached at one end, connects with the combination lever and is attached at the other end to the expansion die block in the link. The raising or lowering of the rear end of the radius rod causes the die block to be raised or lowered in the link.

Normally the bottom of the link is used for fore-gear and the top of the link for back-gear working, giving a direct movement for fore gear and an indirect movement for back gear. The method of reversing is shown in the diagrams of the valve gear.

When the die block is in the centre of the expansion link for mid-gear position, the expansion link does not transfer any movement to the radius rod. Intermediate positions of the expansion die block above or below the centre of the link allow for proportional transfer of movement from the link to the radius rod and valve.

The combined movements of the two sections (*a*) and (*b*) of the gear result in a total movement of the valve equal to twice the

Fig. 46 WALSCHAERT'S VALVE GEAR
Former G.W. Railway
Four-cylinder Locomotives

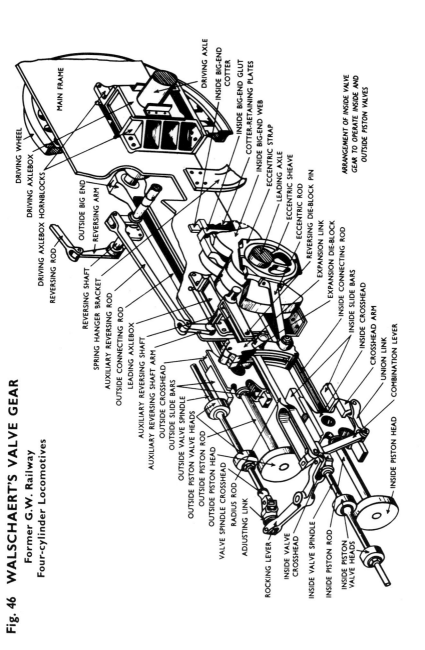

ARRANGEMENT OF INSIDE VALVE GEAR TO OPERATE INSIDE AND OUTSIDE PISTON VALVES

Fig. 46

106

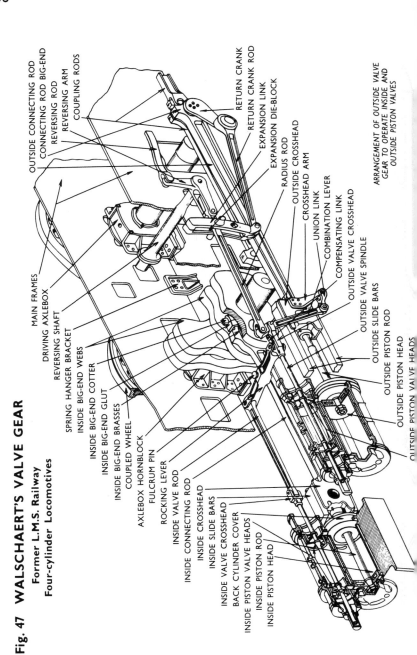

Fig. 47 WALSCHAERT'S VALVE GEAR
Former L.M.S. Railway
Four-cylinder Locomotives

OUTSIDE CONNECTING ROD
CONNECTING ROD BIG-END
REVERSING ROD
REVERSING ARM
COUPLING RODS
RETURN CRANK
RETURN CRANK ROD
EXPANSION LINK
EXPANSION DIE-BLOCK
RADIUS ROD
OUTSIDE CROSSHEAD
CROSSHEAD ARM
UNION LINK
COMBINATION LEVER
COMPENSATING LINK
OUTSIDE VALVE CROSSHEAD
OUTSIDE VALVE SPINDLE
OUTSIDE SLIDE BARS
OUTSIDE PISTON ROD
OUTSIDE PISTON HEAD
OUTSIDE PISTON VALVE HEADS

MAIN FRAMES
DRIVING AXLEBOX
REVERSING SHAFT
SPRING HANGER BRACKET
INSIDE BIG-END WEBS
INSIDE BIG-END COTTER
INSIDE BIG-END GLUT
INSIDE BIG-END BRASSES
COUPLED WHEEL
AXLEBOX HORNBLOCK
FULCRUM PIN
ROCKING LEVER
INSIDE VALVE ROD
INSIDE CONNECTING ROD
INSIDE CROSSHEAD
INSIDE SLIDE BARS
INSIDE VALVE CROSSHEAD
BACK CYLINDER COVER
INSIDE PISTON VALVE HEADS
INSIDE PISTON ROD
INSIDE PISTON HEAD

ARRANGEMENT OF OUTSIDE VALVE GEAR TO OPERATE INSIDE AND OUTSIDE PISTON VALVES

Fig. 47

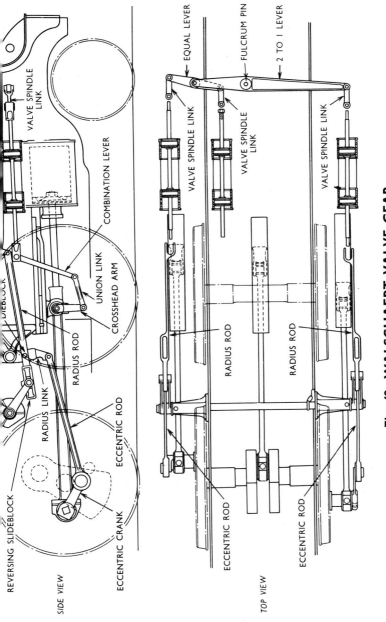

SIDE VIEW

VALVE SPINDLE LINK

COMBINATION LEVER

UNION LINK

CROSSHEAD ARM

RADIUS ROD

ECCENTRIC ROD

RADIUS LINK

REVERSING SLIDEBLOCK

ECCENTRIC CRANK

EQUAL LEVER

FULCRUM PIN

2 TO 1 LEVER

VALVE SPINDLE LINK

VALVE SPINDLE LINK

VALVE SPINDLE LINK

RADIUS ROD

RADIUS ROD

ECCENTRIC ROD

ECCENTRIC ROD

TOP VIEW

Fig. 48 WALSCHAERT VALVE GEAR

(Gresley) former L.N.E. Railway 3-cylinder Locomotives

Fig. 48

Fig. 49 COMBINATION LEVER ARRANGEMENT INSIDE AND OUTSIDE ADMISSION VALVES

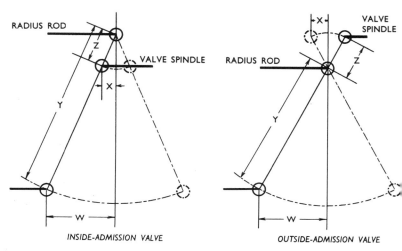

INSIDE-ADMISSION VALVE   OUTSIDE-ADMISSION VALVE

The combination lever is proportioned to move the valve a distance equal to twice the lap plus twice the lead. For inside admission piston valves the following are the essential proportions:—

$$\frac{W}{X} = \frac{Y}{Z}$$

W = Half piston stroke
X = Steam lap plus lead
Y = Length of combination lever
Z = Distance between radius rod and valve spindle connection

For an outside admission valve

Y = Length of combination lever Z

amount of the steam lap plus twice the port opening to steam, for each revolution of the driving wheels.

Rotary Cam Poppet Valve Gear

With reciprocating valve gears of the Stephenson and Walschaert's types, all the valve events of admission, expansion, exhaust and compression are interconnected, as we have previously seen and the evils of early exhaust and compression are always present when working with early cut-offs. To some extent long lap valves allow for short cut-off working.

An improved steam distribution can be obtained by separating valve events so that the admission and cut-off, release and compression are

Fig. 50 ARRANGEMENT OF VALVE GEAR
Former Southern Railway
West Country class locomotives

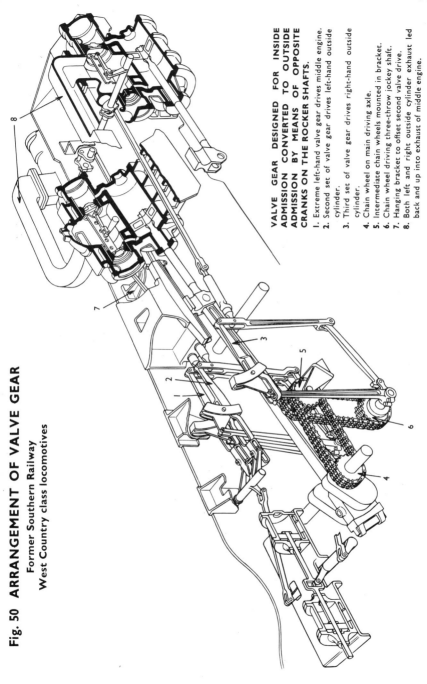

VALVE GEAR DESIGNED FOR INSIDE ADMISSION CONVERTED TO OUTSIDE ADMISSION BY MEANS OF OPPOSITE CRANKS ON THE ROCKER SHAFTS.

1. Extreme left-hand valve gear drives middle engine.
2. Second set of valve gear drives left-hand outside cylinder.
3. Third set of valve gear drives right-hand outside cylinder.
4. Chain wheel on main driving axle.
5. Intermediate chain wheels mounted in bracket.
6. Chain wheel driving three-throw jockey shaft.
7. Hanging bracket to offset second valve drive.
8. Both left and right outside cylinder exhaust led back and up into exhaust of middle engine.

Fig. 50

independent of each other and substantial decrease in back pressure attained with fixed valve events of exhaust and compression for all positions of the reversing gear. The rotary cam poppet valve systems of steam distribution have been designed to achieve this object and allow for a greater expansion of steam, with exhaust and compression periods independent of all the other valve events, thus avoiding wiredrawing by the rapid opening and closing of the ports.

The following is a description of the "British Caprotti" rotary cam poppet valve gear:—

Poppet-type valves, two inlet and two exhaust valves for each cylinder, are provided instead of the normal slide or piston valve. The poppet valves are driven through a form of gear which is totally enclosed and running in oil.

Fig. 51 shows an arrangement of the gear drive, the rotary movement for operating the valves being taken from the return crank gearbox fitted to the driving wheel crank pins. Figs. 52 and 53 show an arrangement where the drive is taken from a gearbox fitted to the leading coupled wheel axle.

In the camboxes are the means of controlling the valve events; Fig. 54 shows a section through the inlet and exhaust valves and a pair of valves are provided at the back and front of double-beat type, the inlet valves being $6\frac{1}{4}$ in. diameter and the exhaust valves 7 in. diameter. Each valve is a self-contained unit within a cage, the exhaust valves being nearest to the locomotive main frames. The valves work vertically in the cages and are pushed down to open.

The valves are operated and guided by the valve spindles on the top of which are caps. The valves are forced up to their seatings by steam acting on the bottom extension of the valve spindles. This steam is used to close the valves all the time the regulator is open and is controlled by means of a small valve in the regulator head.

When the regulator is opened, saturated steam from the regulator head passes through the actuating pipe to the underside of the valve spindle extensions.

A drain valve in the lowest portion of the actuating pipe opens when steam is shut off to prevent the accumulation of water and also to ensure that the valves drop off their seatings immediately the regulator is closed, thereby providing an automatic by-pass between both sides of the piston.

The Cambox

The principal components inside the cambox are the camshaft, with its cams, scrolls, scroll collar, inlet and exhaust levers, swing beams and rollers.

111

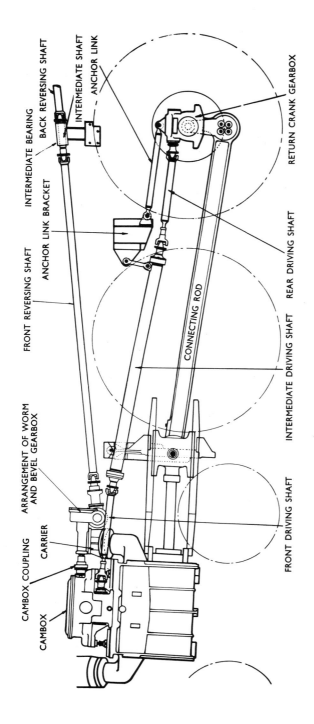

Fig. 51 GENERAL ARRANGEMENT OF BRITISH CAPROTTI VALVE GEAR, OUTSIDE DRIVE

CAMBOX

CAMBOX COUPLING

CARRIER

ARRANGEMENT OF WORM AND BEVEL GEARBOX

FRONT REVERSING SHAFT

ANCHOR LINK BRACKET

INTERMEDIATE BEARING

BACK REVERSING SHAFT

INTERMEDIATE SHAFT

ANCHOR LINK

RETURN CRANK GEARBOX

REAR DRIVING SHAFT

CONNECTING ROD

INTERMEDIATE DRIVING SHAFT

FRONT DRIVING SHAFT

Fig. 51

112

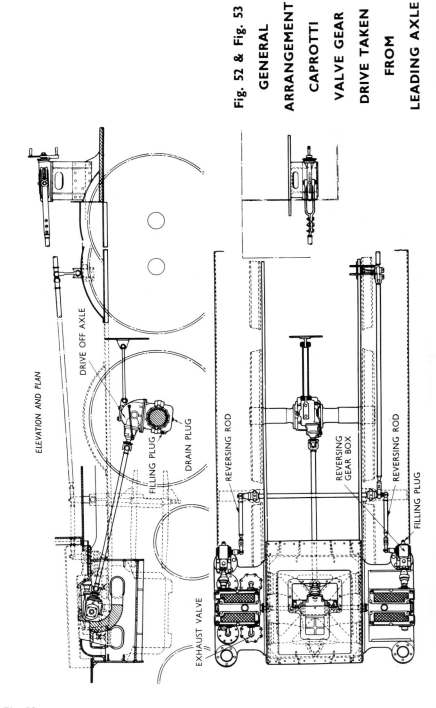

Fig. 52 & Fig. 53
GENERAL
ARRANGEMENT
CAPROTTI
VALVE GEAR
DRIVE TAKEN
FROM
LEADING AXLE

ELEVATION AND PLAN

DRIVE OFF AXLE

FILLING PLUG

DRAIN PLUG

REVERSING ROD

REVERSING GEAR BOX

REVERSING ROD

FILLING PLUG

EXHAUST VALVE

Fig. 52

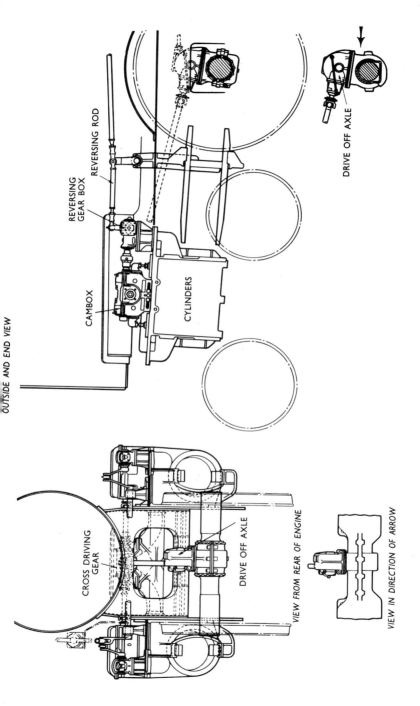

OUTSIDE AND END VIEW

REVERSING ROD

REVERSING GEAR BOX

CAMBOX

CYLINDERS

DRIVE OFF AXLE

CROSS DRIVING GEAR

DRIVE OFF AXLE

VIEW FROM REAR OF ENGINE

VIEW IN DIRECTION OF ARROW

Fig. 53

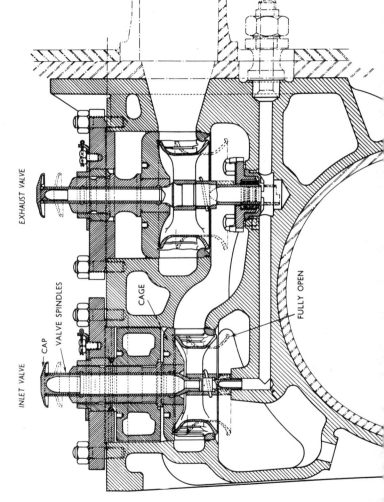

Fig. 54 BRITISH CAPROTTI VALVE GEAR SECTION
THROUGH INLET AND EXHAUST VALVES

EXHAUST VALVE

INLET VALVE

CAP

VALVE SPINDLES

CAGE

FULLY OPEN

Fig. 54

The camshaft, which rotates at engine speed, has the two sets of inlet and exhaust cams loosely mounted. Two separate cams operate through swing beams and tappets, the front and back inlet valves and similarly two separate cams operate the exhaust tappets. Mounted on the camshaft between the two sets of inlet and exhaust cams are two scroll nuts which can rotate and be moved longitudinally along the threaded portion of the camshaft.

The locomotive is reversed by advancing or retarding the angular positions of the cams relative to the camshaft. Any cut-off desired is obtained by angular shifting round of the inlet cams in relation to each other.

Reversing Gear

Reversing is by means of a standard-type reversing screw and handle on footplate movement from two arms on the intermediate cross-shaft being transmitted by two short reversing rods to the gearboxes which finally transmit the reversing motion to the cambox on each cylinder.

INSTRUCTIONS TO FOOTPLATE STAFF

Method of working engines fitted with "Caprotti" valve gear

Two things are absolutely essential in the working of these engines:—

FIRST, THE REGULATORS MUST ALWAYS BE FIRMLY CLOSED WHEN COASTING.

Under these conditions all the valves will fall fully away from their seatings and a full by-pass effect is obtained with the gear *in any position*. There is no necessity to move the gear to find the best coasting position.

Coasting with a breath of steam will cause the valves to chatter, which will adversely affect their efficiency.

Secondly, when reversing from any cut-off in fore gear, it is necessary to wind the reversing screw right back to full back gear. Similarly, when reversing from any position in back gear, the indicator must be traversed to full forward gear position.

The engine will not reverse if the gear is set in some intermediate position.

In all other respects the Caprotti valve gear can be operated in a normal manner, but to obtain the best results *work the engine as much as possible with a full open regulator.*

Defects on the Road

1. *Complete failure of the engine.* This can be caused by fracture of the main driving shaft or its universal joints and couplings, or defects in either the axle drive or in the cross-driver gearbox under the smokebox.

2. *Failure of one side of the engine* will arise from any defect in the cross-driving shafts or couplings between the bevel pinions in the cross-driving gearbox under the smokebox and the cambox or from a defect in one of the camboxes.

3. *Valves sticking and blowing through may be due to:—*
   (a) Valve spindles not working freely in their guides.
   (b) Broken valves and cages or defective valve seatings.
   (c) Leakage or stoppage in actuating steam pipe which supplies steam from the regulator head to the underside of the valve spindle extensions.

Questions and Answers

(1) *Q.* What operates the valves on a locomotive?
   A. The valves are operated by a valve gear which also incorporates an arrangement for regulating the valve travel and for reversing the engine by changing the valve's position on the port face in relation to the piston.

(2) *Q.* Name two common types of valve gears in use.
   A. The Stephenson's link motion; Walschaert's valve gear.

(3) *Q.* Describe the Stephenson's link motion.
   A. This type of motion (illustrated in Figs. 41 and 42) employs two eccentrics for each valve, one being used for forward and the other for backward running. The fore-gear eccentric rod being coupled to the top and the back-gear eccentric rod to the bottom of the curved expansion link, which is supported by lifting links from the reversing shaft. The links and forward ends of the eccentric rods can be raised or lowered by means of a reversing gear in the cab for regulating the cut-off and reversing.

   The expansion link contains an expansion die block, which is coupled to the intermediate valve rod, but on some locomotives having inside-admission piston valves, the drive from the die block is conveyed to the valve spindle through a rocking lever which serves to alter the direction of movement of the valve in relation to the die block.

   On ex-G.W.R. two-cylinder locomotives employing outside cylinders and Stephenson valve gear the valve motion is transmitted from inside the frame to the outside to actuate the piston valve by means of a "rocking shaft" (see Fig. 42). This shaft does not reverse the direction of movement of the valve and the eccentrics are set as in the case of a valve operating piston valves direct.

(4) *Q.* Explain briefly the working of this valve gear.

A. The forward and backward eccentrics are each mounted in their correct position on the axle to drive the valve for the corresponding direction of running, the usual setting being 90° in advance of the crank in the direction of travel to give the necessary port opening plus an angle of advance equal to about 16° to provide a movement to correspond with the lap and lead of the valve. The total advance of each eccentric is approximately 106° in front of the crank in the direction of travel.

In operating the reversing gear the expansion link is raised or lowered in order to bring the expansion die block in line with, or closer to, the backward or forward eccentric rod according to the desired direction of travel and the cut-off required. In full gear positions the expansion link die block will be either at the top or the bottom of the link, in mid gear it will be central where it is acted upon equally by both eccentrics and obtains a travel which is transferred to the valve equal to twice (lead + steam lap).

It is to be noted that the amount of lead given to the valve by the Stephenson's motion is not constant in all positions of the reversing gear. In mid-gear the lead is increased above the amount obtained in full backward or full forward gear (see Fig. 43).

(5) *Q.* Describe an eccentric.

A. The eccentric is a form of auxiliary crank (see Figs. 35 and 35A) used to obtain a reciprocating or to and fro movement for the valves from the crank axle or other rotating part.

It consists of a circular disc called the "sheave" which is securely fixed to the axle so that it will rotate with it. The centre of the sheave does not coincide with the centre of the axle, the distance between these two centres being the amount of eccentricity of the eccentric in the same way as the distance between the crank-pin centre and the axle centre is the "throw" of the ordinary crank.

The eccentricity of the "sheave" causes it to describe a

circular path about the axle centre, and consequently the eccentric strap, which encircles the sheave and works upon its outer surface, is also caused to follow the same circular path, producing a backward and forward movement at the front end of the eccentric rod.

(6) *Q.* Describe a return crank.

    A. The action of the return crank is similar to that of the eccentric sheave (Figs. 35 and 44). It is in the form of an auxiliary crank fitted to the main crank pin at one end and to the return crank rod at the other. The difference between the centre of the axle and centre of eccentric crank pin being the amount of eccentricity as shown.

(7) *Q.* Give a brief description of the Walschaert's valve gear.

    A. In this type of gear (Fig. 45) the valve travel is derived from two separate points. Movement amounting to twice the lap plus twice the lead is obtained from the piston rod crosshead, giving a constant lead for all positions of the gear, the remainder of the valve travel amounting to twice the port opening is obtained from the return crank through the medium of the return crank rod, expansion link, expansion die block and radius rod. The two movements, added together at the valve spindle pin in the combination lever, produce the full travel of the valve with the reversing gear in full forward or full backward position.

    When the expansion die block is in the centre of the link it is in line with the link trunnion pins and consequently no movement will be imparted to the radius rod, the reversing gear being in mid-position. In this position the valve travel is confined to the lap and lead movement obtained from the crosshead drive, the ports being open to the extent of lead only at each end of the cylinder.

    Fore-gear drive for the valve is obtained by lowering the expansion die block below and backward gear by similarly raising it above the link centre.

    Adjustment of the valve travel is controlled from the reversing gear by raising or lowering the expansion die block in the expansion link, regulating the amount and direction of the movement transmitted to the valve spindle from the eccentric or return crank.

(8) *Q.* Why is Walschaert's valve gear fitted to modern locomotives?

    A. Because it possesses a number of important advantages over certain other types. It is readily adapted for use with inside or outside admission valves and for inside or outside cylinders. It is capable of providing a long travel valve which makes for better steam distribution, it only requires one eccentric crank per cylinder and is not complicated, it gives greater facility to examine all parts and is much lighter than other gears.

(9) *Q.* What special points should the Driver bear in mind when working a modern engine fitted with Walschaert's valve gear?

A. That the long valve travel provides the means of taking full advantage of the benefits of expansive working, so that the best results may be obtained with the regulator well opened and the gear pulled up as far as possible, whenever the conditions of working will permit.

(10) *Q.* Are cases of damaged motion or rods common on modern locomotives?

A. No, but a case may arise where a knowledge of failures and remedies would minimise delay to a train and perhaps save the cost of sending for an assisting engine.

(11) *Q.* How would you deal with a broken piston rod?

A. With this failure it is practically certain that the front cylinder cover and piston head will be damaged, but that the piston crosshead, connecting rod and valve motion remain intact. If this is the case all that would be necessary would be to disconnect the valve on that side and secure it centrally over the ports of the affected cylinder.

(12) *Q.* How would you secure the valve central over the ports.

A. The drive must first be disconnected from the valve spindle, which on the Walschaert's gear is readily done by uncoupling the lower end of the combination lever. Uncouple the eccentric rod at the expansion link foot and secure it with the necessary freedom clear of any obstruction—see also Answer 16.

Obtain wooden rail keys and insert the necessary amount of packing to secure the valve spindle guide blocks centrally in the guides. Firmly secure the bottom end of the combination lever as far forward as possible to clear the gudgeon pin when running. It must be noted that this prevents any movement of the reversing gear without first freeing the combination lever.

It would not be necessary to disconnect the motion on the affected side from the reversing shaft. In all cases where engine failures require the dismantling of any detail and securing of other parts the engine should be moved slowly for the first turn to ensure that everything is clear for running.

(13) *Q.* To disconnect a valve on the Walschaert's gear is it necessary to remove the whole of the motion on that side?

A. No, it is only necessary to take down the return crank rod and to remove the union link which connects the crosshead arm to the lower end of the combination lever. The whole of the remaining rods may be left in position, the valve spindle can be secured central over the ports in the manner described previously.

It is unnecessary in this case to uncouple the radius rod from the reversing shaft arm due to the fact that the expansion link will be left swinging free, so that the movement of the reversing shaft will not be transmitted to the valve spindle.

(14) *Q.* What can be done if the radius rod breaks with the Walschaert's gear?

A. Disconnect the affected valve entirely by removing the union link from the crosshead, centralise the valve over the ports and secure as previously described. Tie up the broken portion of the radius rod clear of all moving parts, but do not waste time in trying to remove them. If the engine has not far to run, the connecting rod may be left in position and the cylinder cocks left open. Lubricate the piston generously by working the mechanical lubricator by hand before starting and occasionally during the journey.

(15) *Q.* What would you do if the combination lever broke?

A. Disconnect the affected valve entirely by removal of the return crank rod, centralise and secure the valve as described, then proceed as in previous question when locomotive can be worked on one side to nearest Motive Power Depot.

(16) *Q.* What would you do if the return crank rod broke with the Walschaert's valve gear?

A. Remove the rear portion of the broken rod and tie up the front part clear of moving parts. Disconnect the affected motion from the reversing shaft and then fasten the expansion die block centrally in the expansion link by means of packing. The engine may then be worked on the remaining cylinders with the damaged side working on lead steam only.

In the event of the return crank rod being fitted with ball

bearings, the return crank rod would require to be removed complete and, as the connecting rod big end is retained in position by the return crank, a special washer would be required to be fitted to the main crank pin to retain the connecting rod in position. Assistance would be required from a Motive Power Depot.

If it is an outside motion affected it should be noted that the mechanical lubricators may be put out of action if they are driven from the disconnected link and they must therefore be worked by hand.

(17) Q. If when running in back gear the reversing rod broke, what would occur?

A. In this case the motion would creep into forward gear and the effect noted in the action of the locomotive.

(18) Q. If this occurred what would you do to make the engine fit to proceed?

A. If fitted with Walschaert's gear the reversing shaft arm would have to be levered until the expansion die blocks were raised to the desired position in the links and wooden packing should be inserted in each link below the die block to support it in position. The die blocks should also be packed on the opposite side of the link to prevent any tendency to jump when running. The packing pieces should be securely tied in position with rope or cord to prevent their working out of position.

If the engine were fitted with Stephenson's link motion it would be necessary to lift the links by levering the reversing arms upward until the die blocks are set in a suitable position for running backwards and then to insert wooden packing over each die block to support the links in the desired position. It would be desirable to insert packing below the die blocks also, to prevent any tendency of the links to jump when running, allowing a small vertical movement for slip of link.

(19) Q. If the valve spindle were broken between the heads on an inside-admission piston valve, what would you do?

A. In this case the front head would be driven forward and held at the forward end of the steam chest by the steam pressure, leaving the front port permanently open to steam; probably the quickest remedy in such a case would be to uncouple the valve spindle by removal of the union link and return crank rod on the Walschaert's motion and to draw the rear portion of the valve spindle right back and secure it there in order to open the back port to steam also. This will place the piston in equilibrium with steam at equal pressure front and rear so that the removal of the connecting rod will not be necessary.

With the Stephenson link motion it will be necessary to uncouple the valve spindle by removing the valve link from the rocking or rock shaft.

(20) *Q.* How would you make the engine fit to travel under its own power with a valve spindle broken behind the valve?

   A. In this case the valve would come to rest in its forward position, so that if it were of the outside-admission type the back port would be left open to steam, and if it were an inside-admission valve the front port would be left open. It would be necessary, therefore, to remove the connecting rod and place the piston at the end of the cylinder remote from the open steam port and to secure the piston rod in this position by packing with wood ropes to the slide bar. The back portion of the valve spindle should be pushed against the front portion and wedged in that position to prevent the valve on the port face from moving, also the valve gear, of whatever type, would have to be disconnected from the valve spindle to ensure that no movement would be imparted to the defective valve.

   Note: The former G.W.R. four-cylinder locomotives are fitted with Walschaert's valve gear between the frames and require to be dealt with in a slightly different manner.

(21) *Q.* If one of the outside cylinder pistons became defective, would it be possible to work on three cylinders?

   A. Yes. Disconnect the outside valve at the knuckle joint of the defective side, place piston valve central and secure the adjusting link to prevent it striking the valve spindle.

(22) *Q.* How would you uncouple one of the inside Walschaert's valve gears to make the engine fit to travel?

   A. Take down the combination lever and anchor (guiding) link and place reversing gear in mid-gear. There are three bridle rods to these engines, one from the screw to the reversing shaft and one on each side from the reversing shaft arms to the valve gear. To complete the uncoupling it would be necessary to take down the inside bridle rod on the other faulty side, then using the same pin, couple the auxiliary shaft arm to the emergency bracket fixed on the inside of the framing.

(23) *Q.* If, when running, your locomotive suddenly lost two beats and commenced to ride somewhat roughly, but developed no blow from the chimney, what would you conclude had gone wrong and what would be your procedure under such circumstances?

A. I should conclude that one valve had become uncoupled due to broken valve spindle, eccentric rod or other main portion of the motion. I should at once ease the regulator, open the cylinder cocks and keeping the reversing gear as near to mid-gear as possible (providing the trouble showed no signs of becoming worse) endeavour to bring my train under protection of fixed signals before stopping.

(24) *Q.* How would you deal with a broken back-gear eccentric rod or strap with Stephenson's link motion?

A. If working in fore gear the quickest procedure would be to remove back-gear eccentric rod and strap, drop the reverse into fore gear, secure the link so that the locomotive cannot be reversed and proceed.

Where the lifting link is secured to centre of expansion link, the bottom of the expansion link should be secured to the motion plate to prevent it striking. If necessary to run backwards, the forward eccentric rod and strap will require to be removed, the valve disconnected and secured in mid-position and the locomotive worked on one side.

Other Running Gear Failures

(25) *Q.* In the case of a broken or bent side rod, what should be done?

A. Take down the broken or bent rod or section of rod and the corresponding rod or section of rod on other side of the locomotive. If the front section of six-coupled locomotive's coupling rods became broken or bent all side rods would have to be taken off; similarly, if the middle section of an eight-coupled locomotive's side rod broke, all coupling rods would have to be dismantled.

(26) *Q.* For what breakdown is it necessary to take down the connecting rod and/or side rods?

A. Broken connecting rod, big- or little-end straps, main crank pin, crosshead guide or a defective valve which cannot be closed.

The side rods must be taken down on both sides for broken main crank pin or broken side rod pin.

(27) *Q.* What should be done if a bearing spring dropped, spring badly broken or a broken spring hanger?

    A. Bring the train under such control in order to proceed cautiously to the protection of fixed signals where an examination can be made.

    If the leading spring is broken or lost and the engine is a considerable distance from a Motive Power Depot, as quickly as possible raise the locomotive by running the second pair of wheels, on the same side, on to a suitable packing, such as a steel chisel, coal pick or fishplate placed on the rail, so that the leading end of the engine will be lifted high enough to enable a suitable piece of packing to be inserted on the top of the axlebox affected, then slowly move off the packing on the rail and proceed at reduced speed until a fresh locomotive can be obtained. By this procedure the weight is transmitted direct to the axlebox instead of through the spring. In the event of driving, or any of the other bearing, springs being affected, run the next pair of wheels on to packing on the rail and proceed as for the leading wheel spring.

(28) *Q.* When an engine or tender has been re-railed after derailment, what should the Driver be very careful about?

    A. He should see that the springs, pins and hangers are correct and that no packing has been left on the axleboxes or under-keeps. He should also have the wheels gauged.

    The tender, pony truck or bogie brasses must be examined to see that they are in their proper position and the packing or oil pads are in position.

(29) *Q.* If you discovered that your locomotive had a hot big end and that there was a risk of the metal being fused, how would you handle the engine?

    A. I should keep a breath of steam on at all times and would even bring the train to rest with the regulator open slightly. The cut-off should be maintained as long as possible in order to maintain a more even pressure on the journal and keep the brass in contact with it.

(30) *Q.* Why should you handle the locomotive in this way?

    A. Because, if the metal did fuse in the big-end brasses, the excessive knock might break up the bearing if the steam were shut off. In this event it is possible that one or other of the cylinder covers may be fractured. By keeping a breath of steam on, however, the moving parts are cushioned and damage to the cylinder and piston may possibly be averted.

(31) *Q.* What are some causes for knocks?

A. Driving or coupled wheel axleboxes worn on the bearing or between the horns, worn connecting rod and side rod bushes, worn crossheads, piston rod loose in crosshead, loose piston head, fractured frame or obstruction in the cylinder.

(32) *Q.* How may a knock be usually located?

A. Place locomotive on top or bottom quarter on side to be tested. Reverse from forward to back gear with the regulator open, noting the movement of the axleboxes, connecting rod and side rod bushes, crosshead and piston rod. Ensure the cylinder is not working loose on the frame.

(33) *Q.* What point do you regard as of special importance in connection with sand gear?

A. That the sand boxes on each side of the locomotive are filled and that the ends of the sand pipe nozzle are properly adjusted to deliver the sand between the tread of the wheel and the face of the rail. Both sanders must work simultaneously, for if only one sander is working there is a grave risk of broken coupling rods and crank pins.

(34) *Q.* Would you apply sand to the rail when the locomotive is slipping and the regulator open?

A. No. To avoid sudden strains on the motion the regulator must be closed and slipping have ceased before applying the sand.

SECTION 7

LUBRICATION

Lubricating oil is used to keep the bearing surfaces apart and permit easy running and reduced wear and tear. This is brought about by forming a film or layer of oil between the bearing and shaft or between the sliding surfaces to prevent metallic contact. When oil is allowed to spread over a clean metallic surface it forms a thin film of great stability. This film may be only 100,000th of an inch in thickness, but it adheres strongly to the metal and two such films, one on each surface, slide over each other and protect the metals from contact and wear. "Oiliness" is the property of a liquid which enables it to form a powerful lubricating film when spread as a layer between the two surfaces.

When a locomotive is working, the chief kinds of motion are:—

    (1) Rotating—as in axle and big-end bearings.

    (2) Sliding—as in pistons, crossheads and valves.

    (3) Rocking—as in parts of a valve gear and little-end bearings.

In the first of these types it is easier to maintain a fluid film as the rotation assists the distribution of the oil, but in the other two cases it is more difficult. For example, a piston slows down and stops at the end of each stroke and reverses direction; again, a small end has only a limited amount of movement. Under these conditions, which are unfavourable to the maintenance of a fluid film, we depend upon the "oiliness" of the lubricant to prevent metallic contact.

Methods of Lubrication

A. *Hand Lubrication*

    Example: Hand brake gear, firedoor slides, screw couplings, etc.

    Description: Oil is applied by a hand oil feeder daily or as required.

B. *Pad Lubrication (Worsted)*

    Example: Chiefly used in underkeeps of axleboxes.

    Description: The worsted pad is supplied with oil by tail feeders attached to the pad and dipping into a bath of oil in the underkeeps.

C. *Syphon Lubrication*

    Example: Axleboxes, slide bars, horn cheeks, etc.

    Description: The oil is fed to the bearing or surface from an oil box by means of a worsted tail trimming (see **Fig. 55**).

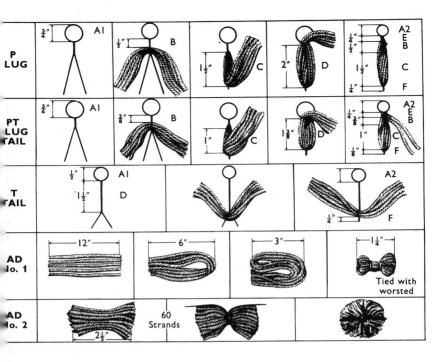

Fig. 55 WORSTED TRIMMINGS
Details of Preparation

D. *Mechanical Lubrication*
Example: Axleboxes, pistons, valves and cylinders, etc.
Description: Lubrication is effected by means of a mechanical pump (see Figs. 56 and 57).

E. *Hydrostatic Sight Feed Lubrication*
Example: Valves, pistons and cylinders.
Description: Lubricators of this type work on the principle of the displacement of oil by means of condensed steam (see Fig. 58).

F. *Atomised Lubrication*
Example: Valves, pistons and cylinders.
Description: With both mechanical and sight feed lubricators the oil is atomised with steam and sprayed through a choke

before it reaches the cylinders. In some systems of mechanical lubrication, steam to the atomisers is controlled automatically from the cylinder cock gear (see Fig. 59).

G. *Restrictor Plug Lubrication*

Example: Big ends and side rod bushes.

Description: On revolving parts, the oil supply tube in the oil well is fitted with either a worsted trimming, a screwed metal restrictor or a needle. These devices regulate the quantity of oil passing down the oil tube, the oil being thrown to the top of the oil tube by the movement of the part concerned (see Fig. 60).

H. *Fountain-type Lubrication*

Example: Axleboxes on a small number of classes of locomotives.

Description: This lubricator feeds oil by gravity to the axleboxes and consists of an airtight oil reservoir which supplies oil to a feed chamber through a main shut-off valve. The level of the air in the chamber controls the admission of air to the reservoir, thereby regulating the delivery of oil from it. Oil leaves the feed chambers through drip nozzles, the flow being regulated by feed needles and passes through sight feed glasses into the oil pipes, thence by gravity to the axleboxes (see Fig. 61).

I. *Grease Lubrication*

Example: Ball and roller bearings, return crank, motion parts, brake gearings, water pick-up gearings, pony trucks, reversing screw, etc.

Description: Grease nipples are screwed into each lubricating point, being sealed with a spring-loaded valve to prevent dirt getting into the hole. A grease gun is used to force lubricant through the nipples to the point of lubrication.

Lubrication of Axleboxes

Locomotive axleboxes can be divided into two types, viz. (*a*) dead load bearings as fitted to bogie, pony truck, bissel trucks and tenders; (*b*) dead load-power bearings, as on the driving and coupled wheels, which in addition to taking the dead weight are also called upon to transmit a considerable proportion of the piston thrust to the locomotive frames to form the tractive force.

On modern locomotives the former type of bearing depends entirely on oil supplied by the underfeed keep pad, and care must be taken during preparation to check the underkeep oil level.

With coupled wheels, although oil can be supplied to the bearing by mechanical lubricator or trimming feed, the method of applying the oil to the actual bearing surface varies, but the following are in common use:—

(1) By a straight oil groove cut on crown of bearing.

(2) By oval groove on crown of bearing.

(3) By straight oil grooves at 45° on each side of the vertical centre line of bearing.

(4) By oil holes on horizontal centre line of bearing.

(5) Plain whitemetal bearing with underfeed keep lubrication (latest practice).

A number of locomotives are being fitted with roller bearings on all axles. The advantages of these are lower lubricating costs and lower resistance when starting from rest.

Where mechanical lubrication is employed a spring-loaded back-pressure valve is fitted on the axlebox, whose function is to keep the oil supply pipe full whilst the locomotive is standing, so that the oil supply commences immediately the locomotive moves.

With bearings as described in item (5) the oil supply is mechanically fed to the underkeep.

Mechanical Lubricators

The Silvertown mechanical lubricator consists of a cast-iron box into which is fitted a number of independent oil pumps, all of which are operated simultaneously. The box itself forms an oil container and is fitted with a hinged lid for the purpose of replenishing the oil, which is filtered through a fine-mesh sieve (Fig. 56).

The supply pumps are double acting, oil is delivered on both the up and down movements of the pump plunger, giving a continuous oil supply. The lubricator is driven from some convenient point on the motion through a ratchet wheel which drives the shaft in one direction. On each end of the shaft is a cam working in slots in the driving frame, the latter being so arranged to slide vertically in guides at each end of the lubricating box. When the driving shaft revolves a reciprocating motion is given to the frame which is connected to the pump plunger by means of thimbles.

The action of the pump is as follows:—

On the upward movement of the plunger, oil is drawn via a small sieve past a ball valve, thus filling the space below the plunger. During the downward movement of the plunger the ball valve is held on its seat and the oil is forced up the passage past the ball valve, half of the oil filling the cavity on the top of the plunger and the

Fig. 56 SILVERTOWN MECHANICAL LUBRICATOR

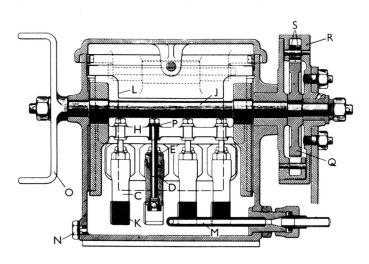

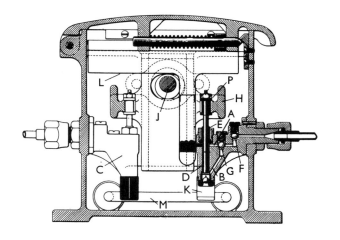

A. CAVITY	K. SMALL SIEVE
B. PASSAGE	L. FINE-MESH SIEVE
C. SUPPLY PUMPS	M. WARMING PIPE
D. PUMP PLUNGER	N. DRAIN PLUG
E. PACKING	O. DRIVING SHAFT HANDLE
F. BALL VALVE	P. THIMBLES
G. BALL VALVE	Q. DRIVING WHEEL
H. DRIVING FRAME	R. FIXED WHEEL PLATE
J. SHAFT	S. PAWL

remaining oil being forced past the ball valve into the lubricating system. It will be seen that on the upward movement, in addition to the oil being drawn into the lower passages of the pump, the oil remaining in the cavity is also forced past the ball valve, during which operation the ball valve is held on its seat. Special packing is provided to prevent leakage of oil from the top side of the plunger.

The rotary movement of the shaft is obtained by six spring-loaded pawls fitted to the outer case of the ratchet box and engaging in teeth on the outside edge of the driving wheel which is keyed to the main shaft, so that when the case is moving in one direction the driving wheel is rotated, but in the return direction is held in position by means of the six retaining pawls provided in the fixed wheel plate.

Each pump feeds approximately 2 oz. per 100 miles.

On the opposite end of the driving shaft a handle is fitted which can be turned by hand to operate the pump independent of the action of the locomotive. This handle should be rotated a few times before leaving the shed.

These lubricators can be used to supply oil to the axleboxes or to the cylinders. When used for the latter purpose, as a thick oil is used for cylinder lubrication, it is necessary to provide means for preventing the oil from congealing in cold weather and this is achieved by fitting a warming pipe through which a supply of steam is passed. This supply of steam can be cut off during the summer weather. When necessary the oil can be drained from the lubricator through a drain plug.

Hydrostatic Displacement Lubricator

The principle of the hydrostatic displacement lubricator is the utilisation of condensed steam from the condenser coil, which on entering the oil reservoir displaces the oil causing it to overflow into the feed passages. Oil is controlled by the oil-regulating valve and, after passing this point, it rises through the water in the sight glass into a delivery chamber from which it is carried by steam through the lubricator pipes to the choke which is inserted in the lubricator pipe near the delivery point on the main steam pipes. The choke plug gives a constant resistance to the lubricator and so prevents the feed being affected by variations of pressure in the steam chest.

On the former G.W.R. locomotives the oil is atomised by passing through a small orifice from the delivery chamber.

The usual rate of feed should be two to three drops per feed per minute, according to the class of work performed.

A Detroit hydrostatic lubricator is shown in Fig. 58. This is a four-feed lubricator and the working instructions are as follows:—

To fill: Turn oil control valve to closed position. Shut water valve and steam valve, open the drain plug in order to empty water from oil reservoir and release pressure, next remove filling plug slowly. (The reason for removing this plug slowly is to allow any pressure which may have built up in the reservoir to escape past the threads.) Close the drain plug and fill reservoir with clean oil; if there is insufficient oil on hand use water to fill reservoir completely. (Some lubricators of this type are not fitted with oil control valve; in this case when filling close all feed regulating valves.)

To start: Fully open the steam valve and allow three or four minutes to elapse in which to fill the condenser and sight feed glasses with water, then fully open water valve, turn oil control valve to "open" position and regulate the oil feed valves.

To shut down lubricator: For short stops shut down oil control valve only; for long stops close oil control valve, water valve and lastly steam valve.

Note: Always start the lubricator ten minutes before leaving the shed.

Fig. 57 WAKEFIELD MECHANICAL LUBRICATOR
No. 7 Pattern

HOW THE LUBRICATOR WORKS

When the pump plunger **D** and sleeve valve **E** are at the outer end of the stroke, oil flows into the pump barrel **C** through the ports **F**. As soon as the ports **F** are covered by the plunger and sleeve valve on the return stroke, the oil in the pump barrel is forced away under pressure to the outlets **K**. If the oil regulating plug **G** is screwed right down, the pumps are working at their full capacity. One full turn outwards of the oil regulating plug **G** decreased the oil pumped by one-fifth as follows:—

Plug **G** screwed right down	= full feed.
Plug **G** screwed one turn out	= four-fifths feed
Plug **G** screwed two turns out	= three-fifths feed
Plug **G** screwed three turns out	= two-fifths feed
Plug **G** screwed four turns out	= one-fifth feed
Plug **G** screwed five turns out	= feed cut off

TO OPERATE

When starting the Lubricator for the first time when newly fitted—
(1) See that each of the oil regulating plugs **G** is screwed right down.
(2) Fill the oil reservoir, taking care to pass the oil through the strainer.
(3) Open the oil-test plug on the combined check valve and oil-test plug.
(4) Work the Lubricator by turning the flushing wheel until the oil is seen at the oil-test plug.
(5) Close the oil-test plug and work the Lubricator a few more times to make sure that the oil-delivery pipes are quite full.

The above operations are essential when the lubrication is first fitted up. The lubrication system is then in working order.

It is advisable before leaving the shed, with the engine going into traffic, to examine the test plugs and make sure the oil is there by giving the flushing wheel a few turns.

The level of the oil in the reservoir must never be allowed to fall below the ports **F** in the pump barrels or no oil will be delivered.

The oil MUST pass through the sieve. It is advantageous to WARM the cylinder oil before filling the lubricator.

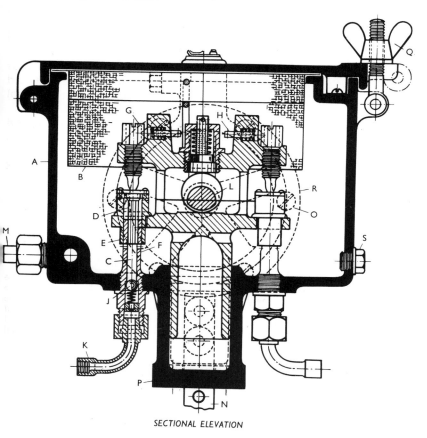

SECTIONAL ELEVATION

A. OIL RESERVOIR
B. WIRE GAUZE STRAINER
C. PUMP BARREL
D. PUMP PLUNGER
E. SLEEVE VALVE
F. OIL PORTS
G. OIL REGULATING PLUG
H. OIL REGULATING LOCKING PEG
J. NON-RETURN VALVE

K. OIL OUTLETS
L. DRIVING ECCENTRIC SHAFT
M. OIL WARMING PIPE
N. DRIVING ARM
O. RATCHET DRIVE AND GEAR CASE
P. FIXING LUGS
Q. FLY BOLT TO SECURE LID
R. FLUSHING WHEEL
S. DRAIN PLUG

NOTE.—No. 7 (a) pattern operates in a similar manner to the above, but the oil outlets K lead out from the sides of the oil reservoir, level with the centre of the driving eccentric shaft L.

Fig. 58 DETROIT HYDROSTATIC SIDE FEED LUBRICATOR

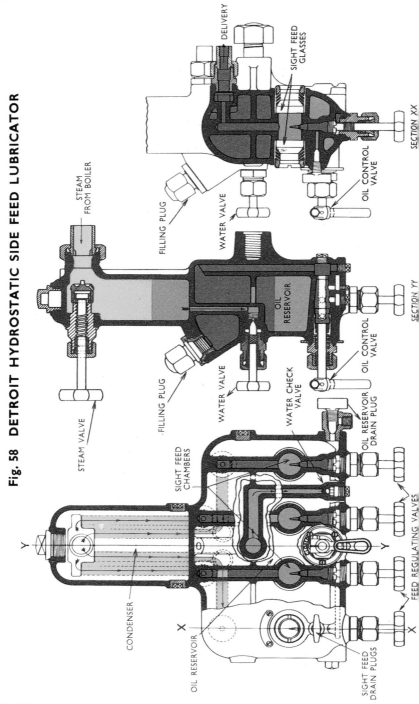

Fig. 58

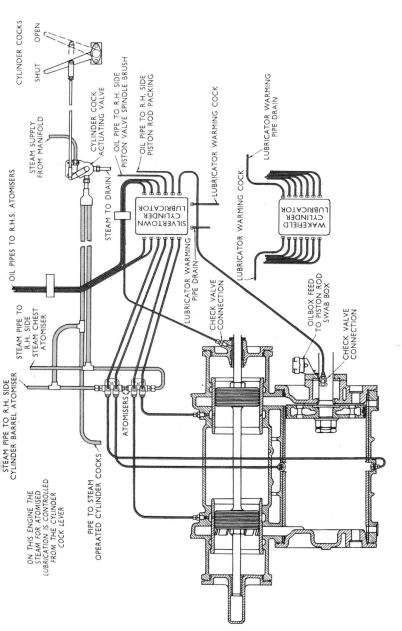

Fig. 59 ARRANGEMENT OF ATOMISER LUBRICATION

Fig. 59

Fig. 60 CONNECTING ROD LUBRICATION

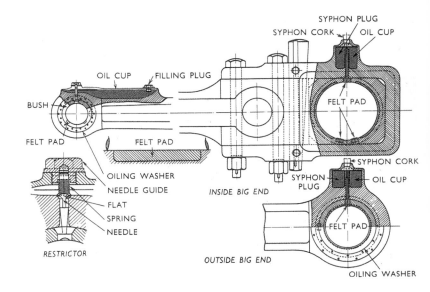

FOUNTAIN-TYPE AXLEBOX LUBRICATOR

INSTRUCTIONS FOR OPERATING

TO FILL Set handle "P" in "OFF" position.
Remove filling plug "B" and fill reservoir with *clean* oil.
Replace filling plug "B" making sure that it is screwed down and air tight.

TO OPERATE Examine needles "J" to see that they are clean, and that no foreign matter is accumulated around or in the nipples "V."
Then replace needles "J" and move handle "P" to "ON" position.

SPECIAL NOTE Handle "P" has two positions, "ON" and "OFF." It does not regulate the oil feed. Feed regulation is obtained by varying the size of needle "J."
NO OIL MUST BE POURED INTO CHAMBER "F."
Lid on chamber "F" is for inspection purposes only.
Move handle "P" into "OFF" position when running into terminal stations, or during any lengthy stoppage.
Do not move handle "P" into the "ON" position until the steam regulator is again opened. The small quantity of oil accumulating in each chamber "G" from feed chamber "F" flows quickly down the oil pipes to the journals immediately the Lubricator is set to work again.
When shunting, operate Lubricator at intervals sufficient to maintain an oil film on the journals.
Should an Axle-box heat, remove needle "J" of the Axle-box feed concerned to temporarily increase the oil delivery until conditions improve, then replace needle "J" or fit a smaller size needle.

TO DETECT STOPPAGE IN PIPE LINE Should oil flood sight glass, it indicates that the feed pipe is choked between the Lubricator and the air inlet in the pipe line.
If oil appears at the air inlet in the pipe line it denotes an obstruction in the pipe between the air inlet and Axle-box.
Air inlets should be periodically examined and kept free from dirt.

HOW IT FUNCTIONS When handle "P" is set in the "ON" position, oil from the reservoir "A" passes through main shut-off valve "C" and along passage "D" into feed chamber "F," where it rises to a level just above top of outlet passage "D" and is fed through the nozzle "L" in drops regulated by the needle "J" fitted in the nipple "V."

As soon as the oil level in chamber "F" drops below top of passage "D," air enters the reservoir "A" through the air tube "T," destroys the partial vacuum, permits the oil to flow through until it again rises to a level above the top of passage "D" and cuts off the air.

This cycle of operations is repeated the whole time the handle "P" is in the "ON" position.

When handle "P" is in the "OFF" position, the main shut-off valve "C" and shut-off valves "K" are closed, and oil in the chamber "F" continues to feed to each auxiliary chamber "G" until the oil level in chamber "F" falls to the level of the top of the nipple "V."

Immediately handle "P" is set in the "ON" position the oil accumulated in each chamber "G" quickly flows down the pipes to the journals, while the cycle of operations between the reservoir "A" and chamber "F" has allowed the level in chamber "F" to rise and feed oil past the needle "J." The air tube "T" regulates the expansion or contraction, due to variation of temperature in reservoir "A."

By strictly observing the above instructions, an appreciable economy in oil consumption will be effected.

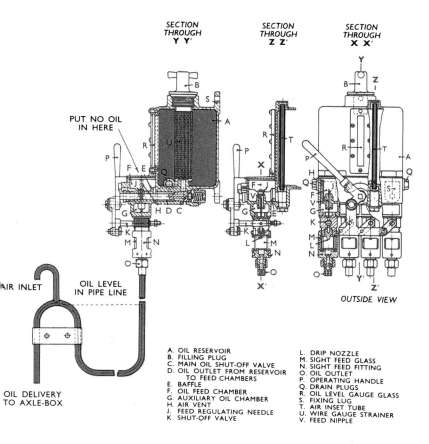

A. OIL RESERVOIR
B. FILLING PLUG
C. MAIN OIL SHUT-OFF VALVE
D. OIL OUTLET FROM RESERVOIR TO FEED CHAMBERS
E. BAFFLE
F. OIL FEED CHAMBER
G. AUXILIARY OIL CHAMBER
H. AIR VENT
J. FEED REGULATING NEEDLE
K. SHUT-OFF VALVE

L. DRIP NOZZLE
M. SIGHT FEED GLASS
N. SIGHT FEED FITTING
O. OIL OUTLET
P. OPERATING HANDLE
Q. DRAIN PLUGS
R. OIL LEVEL GAUGE GLASS
S. FIXING LUG
T. AIR INSET TUBE
U. WIRE GAUGE STRAINER
V. FEED NIPPLE

Fig. 61 FOUNTAIN-TYPE AXLEBOX LUBRICATOR

Roller Bearings

With a view to obtaining economies brought about by more trouble-free running and increased mileages between shop repairs, roller bearings are being fitted to locomotives in increasing numbers, especially to axlebox bearings.

Roller-bearing Axleboxes

Fig. 62 illustrates typical inside and outside journal roller-bearing axleboxes. The bearings used in these axleboxes consist of four main components as follows:—

1. CONE (inner race). The cone is pressed on the axle and therefore rotates with the axle.
2. CUP (outer race). The cup is loosely mounted in the axlebox body, but does not rotate.
3. ROLLERS. The rollers transmit the journal load of the vehicle from the outer to the inner race and roll along the track on the cone.
4. CAGE. The cage ensures that the rollers are correctly spaced.

A. This illustrates an axlebox for outside journals as used on certain trailing truck and tender axles. It includes a double bearing, which in effect is two single sets of rollers running on two single cones.

B. This illustrates an axlebox for outside journals as used on certain tender axles. It includes a double bearing, which, in effect, is two single sets of rollers running on a double cone.

C. This illustrates a cast-steel axlebox as used for inside journals and is known as a "cannon box". It includes two single bearings, one per journal, mounted in a tubular steel housing which entirely surrounds the axle throughout its length between the wheel bosses. Earlier designs of cannon boxes were made in two halves bolted together, but the latest type consists of a solid one-piece tubular casting.

The construction of these bearings, where tapered rollers run on the tapered working surfaces of a cone and cup, makes it equally suitable for handling loads at right-angles to the axle (radial loads such as spring loads, brake loads and piston loads) and thrust loads set up along the axle when the vehicle is negotiating curves in the track. Only the upper rollers carry radial load, whereas all the rollers carry thrust load.

The bearings are lubricated by oil which is automatically circulated in the axlebox by the action of the tapered rollers. Oil level, which is checked with a gauge, should be topped up with the correct grade of oil when the level is down to the lower mark on the gauge.

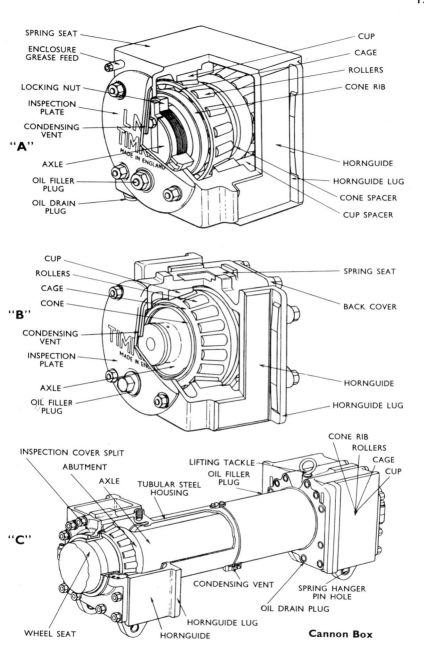

Fig. 62 TYPES OF ROLLER-BEARING AXLEBOXES

This work is carried out by artisan staff, but Enginemen should note that the entry of dirt or water into the axlebox would prove extremely harmful to the bearings.

A condensing vent is cast in the inspection cover of axleboxes (A and B), whilst a condensing vent pipe is fitted to cannon boxes (C). This vent allows the axlebox to "breathe" when the air inside the axlebox expands and contracts.

With a roller bearing the loads are handled on rolling surfaces similar to a wheel rolling on a rail, not on a sliding surface as when a weight is dragged along a road. This is the important difference between a roller bearing and a plain bearing. The friction in the bearing is very small and therefore the tractive resistance or resistance to free running is very low. At starting some of the power developed by a locomotive is absorbed as friction in a plain bearing axlebox and is lost. This loss is almost eliminated on a roller-bearing-equipped locomotive; it can therefore develop more useful tractive effort.

Atomiser Lubrication

From the cylinder mechanical lubricator oil is forced by the pump to the atomiser (Fig. 59), where it is atomised by means of a steam jet and then passed to the steam chest. The steam for atomisers is taken from the manifold. The steam pipe also includes a valve coupled to the cylinder cock gear, which is shut when the cylinder cocks are open. For this reason it is imperative that the cylinder cocks be left open whilst the locomotive is standing.

Questions and Answers

(1) *Q.* Why is the cylinder oil issued for the piston and valves of non-superheated engines different from that issued for superheated engines?

A. The oil used in the latter for lubricating the valves and pistons must be able to retain its lubricating properties at higher temperatures than is necessary with saturated steam.

(2) *Q.* Describe the use of worsted trimmings.

A. A plug trimming is used to feed rotating and oscillating parts having sufficient motion to splash the oil over the end of the syphon tube when the locomotive is in motion. Big ends, outside rods, eccentrics and in small ends of older types of locomotives.

A plug trimming is made by wrapping several strands of worsted lengthwise over a length of twisted wire and forming a plug, which should be a comfortable fit in the syphon tube, and when in position the top of the plug should reach a little below the top of the syphon tube to form a well to accommodate a small quantity of oil above the trimming. The extreme length of the plug should be shorter than the length of the tube to obviate it touching the bearing.

Although, within certain limits, the amount of oil fed will vary according to the number of strands in the plug, care must be taken to adhere to the standard as too many strands may restrict the passage of oil to the bearing.

Tail trimmings are used for non-rotating parts such as axleboxes, piston and valve spindle glands, etc., and they are made of the same material as plug trimmings, the strands being left of sufficient length to fit the syphon tube and hang into the oil box to syphon the oil from the oil chamber to the syphon tube when in position, the oil falling from the trimming in the tube by gravity to the point to be lubricated. The number of strands, within certain limits, will increase the supply of oil with the increase in strands, provided they are kept clean. Tail trimmings should be removed from the syphon tube, when not required, to avoid waste of oil.

Other trimmings in the form of a pad are used for expansion die blocks, expansion link pins and side blocks; these pads being saturated with oil each time the locomotive is prepared, the oil lubricating the part slowly during the time of working.

SECTION 8

BRAKES

The function of the brake is to absorb by friction the momentum of the train; in other words, the energy stored in the moving train is converted to heat at the brake blocks when the brakes are applied.

In the working of freight and mineral trains not made up of power-braked vehicles, the braking of the train is dependent upon the brakes of the locomotive together with the screw hand brake on the guard's brake van, supplemented on certain sections of the line, where there are severe gradients, by stopping the train and applying the hand brake on a number of vehicles before descending the incline.

For the working of passenger trains it is necessary, in order to comply with an Act of Parliament passed in 1889, that (1) the brake on the train should be continuous and capable of being applied to every vehicle of the train; (2) be instantaneous in action and capable of being applied by Driver and/or Guard; (3) be self-applying in the event of the train becoming divided.

These conditions are fulfilled by the two main braking systems in common use to-day, namely, the "automatic vacuum brake" and the "Westinghouse automatic air brake".

The "automatic vacuum brake" is used almost exclusively on steam-hauled trains in this country and makes use of the atmospheric pressure.

The system consists essentially of an exhausting device on the engine known as the vacuum ejector, which has a large ejector used to create quickly the regulation amount of vacuum in the train pipe, connections and reservoir and both sides of the brake cylinder pistons throughout the train, together with a small ejector to maintain the vacuum. Some locomotives are fitted with a vacuum pump which serves a similar purpose to the small ejector.

The pressure of the atmosphere is approximately 15 lb. per sq. in. and the vacuum is measured in inches of mercury. A perfect vacuum corresponds to approximately 30 in. of mercury, i.e. 0 lb. per sq. in. pressure. This varies slightly with the atmospheric pressure as measured by a barometer. Therefore, it will be evident that each 2 in. of vacuum represents approximately 1 lb. per sq. in. of atmospheric pressure.

The regulation vacuum for working the brakes is 21 in. on all Regions except the former G.W.R., where the amount is 25 in.

To apply the brakes, air is admitted to the train pipe and train pipe connections so that the vacuum on the lower side of each brake piston is partially or completely destroyed. The vacuum on the reservoir and upper sides of the brake pistons, however, is retained, being sealed off by a ball valve.

In a normal application of the brakes the Driver can admit the desired amount of air to the train pipe by way of the ports in the Driver's application valve, the quantity of air admitted regulating the power of the application. Full power is utilised when the vacuum in the train pipe is totally destroyed.

Some arrangements of the automatic vacuum brake are worked in conjunction with steam brakes on the engine and tender or in conjunction with the steam brake on the engine only and vacuum brake on the tender.

The arrangement which has been adopted on B.R. standard steam locomotives is shown in Fig. 63. In this arrangement steam brakes are fitted to both engine and tender, the combined ejector (Fig. 64) is separate from the Driver's brake application valve and is placed alongside the left-hand side of the boiler outside the cab. The body contains two ejectors, a large ejector and a small ejector, the action of the large and small ejectors is similar, the difference being that the large ejector uses more steam and thus is capable of creating a vacuum more quickly and therefore is for use when standing or when a quick release of the brake is essential. The small ejector is provided for maintaining the vacuum throughout the train and for overcoming the effect of leakage of air into the vacuum system due to faulty joints at the pipe connections, etc., on the train. Each ejector is fitted with a non-return valve. These two valves, together with the non-return valve and drain connection (Fig. 63), provide an air lock so as to prevent smokebox gases being drawn back through the ejector exhaust. Each ejector works in the following manner:—

Steam passing through the steam cone (Fig. 64) at great velocity is discharged into the ejector air cone where it comes into frictional contact with the air, the steam and air being exhausted through the ejector exhaust pipe and up the engine chimney via the smokebox elbow.

In consequence of this action a partial vacuum is created and any air in the train pipe and connections, in its endeavour to destroy the vacuum created, lifts the non-return valves and finds its way to the ejector where it is discharged together with the steam through the ejector exhaust, thus a vacuum in the train pipe and connections is created.

144

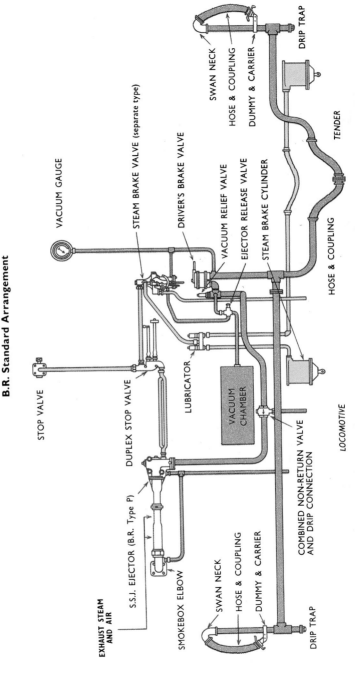

Fig. 63 GENERAL ARRANGEMENT OF
VACUUM AUTOMATIC BRAKE ON ENGINE AND TENDER

B.R. Standard Arrangement

VACUUM GAUGE

STEAM BRAKE VALVE (separate type)

DRIVER'S BRAKE VALVE

VACUUM RELIEF VALVE

EJECTOR RELEASE VALVE

STEAM BRAKE CYLINDER

SWAN NECK

HOSE & COUPLING

DUMMY & CARRIER

DRIP TRAP

TENDER

HOSE & COUPLING

LOCOMOTIVE

STOP VALVE

DUPLEX STOP VALVE

LUBRICATOR

VACUUM CHAMBER

COMBINED NON-RETURN VALVE
AND DRIP CONNECTION

EXHAUST STEAM
AND AIR

S.S.J. EJECTOR (B.R. Type P)

SMOKEBOX ELBOW

SWAN NECK

HOSE & COUPLING

DUMMY & CARRIER

DRIP TRAP

Fig. 63

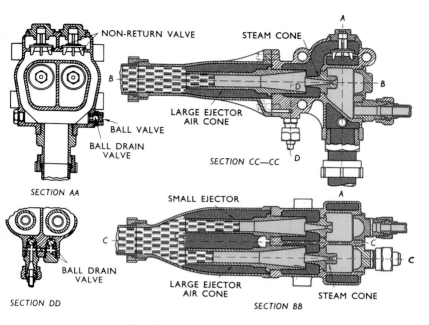

NON-RETURN VALVE   STEAM CONE

LARGE EJECTOR
AIR CONE

BALL VALVE

BALL DRAIN
VALVE

SECTION CC—CC

SECTION AA

SMALL EJECTOR

BALL DRAIN
VALVE

SECTION DD

LARGE EJECTOR
AIR CONE

STEAM CONE

SECTION BB

Fig. 64   S.S.J. EJECTOR

Under each ejector, ball drain valves are provided; whilst the ejectors are in use the ball is forced to its seating, preventing air entering; when the steam supply is shut off, the ball falls away from the seating and allows any condensation to drain away. A ball valve is provided so that in the event of leakage taking place in either of the non-return valves, the ball valve will open to the atmosphere and smokebox gases will not be drawn back through the ejectors when they shut off, but the vacuum maintained in the train pipe.

Driver's brake application valve is shown in Fig. 65 and is designed to admit air into the train pipe so as to reduce or destroy the vacuum. It has only two handle positions, "off" and "on".

Vacuum-operated graduable steam brake valve. This arrangement is shown in Fig. 66 and is designed to admit steam to the steam brake cylinders as the train pipe vacuum is reduced or destroyed and to release the steam from the steam brake cylinders as the train pipe vacuum is restored; in action the brake is applied on the engine and tender slightly later and released slightly earlier than the vacuum

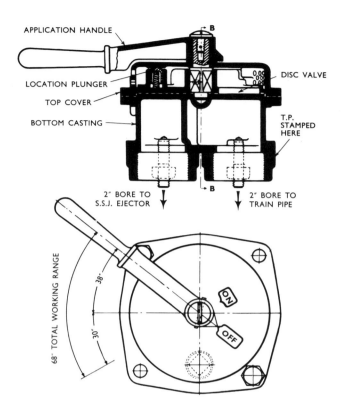

APPLICATION HANDLE

LOCATION PLUNGER

TOP COVER

BOTTOM CASTING

DISC VALVE

T.P. STAMPED HERE

2" BORE TO S.S.J. EJECTOR

2" BORE TO TRAIN PIPE

68" TOTAL WORKING RANGE

38°

30°

ON

OFF

Fig. 65   DRIVER'S BRAKE APPLICATION VALVE
B.R. Standard Locomotive

brake on the train in order to minimise bunching of the carriages and strain on the engine and tender draw-gear; moreover, the pressure of steam in the steam brake cylinder is proportional to the amount by which the vacuum in the train pipe is reduced.

Vacuum relief valve. This is provided to prevent the regulation vacuum being exceeded (see Fig. 63). It consists of a spring-loaded valve which lifts and allows air into the train pipe if the ejectors create more than 21 in. of vacuum (25 in. in the case of the former G.W.R.).

Operation. The operation of brake arrangement as fitted to B.R. standard locomotives (see Fig. 63) is as follows: when in the normal running position the train pipe will be registering 21 in. of vacuum, which will be maintained at this amount by the small ejector. Any over-creation which the small ejector might manage, if not satisfactorily adjusted, will be taken care of by the vacuum relief valve. There will be the normal train pipe vacuum below the vacuum cylinder piston (Fig. 66) due to the direct connection of the

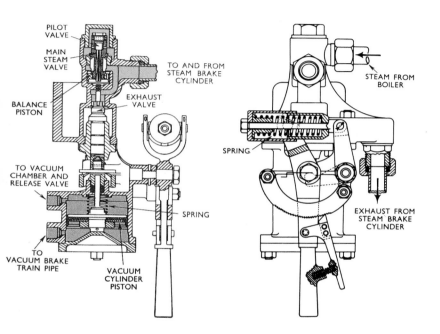

Fig. 66 VACUUM-OPERATED
GRADUABLE STEAM BRAKE VALVE
(Mark IV)

bottom of the vacuum cylinder to the train pipe. On the upper side of the piston there will also be a normal vacuum due to the connection of the upper portion of the piston with the vacuum chamber through the ejector release valve, and the piston will be at its lowest position due to the action of the spring. Steam at boiler pressure is supplied to the chamber above the two valves and the steam brake cylinders are empty of steam, the cylinders being open to atmosphere past the exhaust valve.

When the Driver's brake valve is moved towards the "on" position, the vacuum in the train pipe is reduced due to air being admitted through the brake valve. This also admits air to the underside of vacuum cylinder piston which moves upward, causing the steam brake cylinder exhaust valve to close. Further movement next raises the pilot valve to admit steam below the balance piston which causes it to lift, thus allowing the main steam valve to open and pass steam direct to the steam brake cylinder. This condition continues until the steam pressure in the steam brake cylinder, acting downwards on the exhaust valve, is just sufficient to overcome the upward pressure on the vacuum cylinder piston, which is then forced down until the valves close.

Further downward movement of the air piston, when the vacuum in the train pipe is re-created, permits the steam brake exhaust valve to open and release steam from the brake cylinders to exhaust.

Manual Operation. Manual operation of the steam brake only, for use when running light engine or when working an unbraked train, is carried out by means of a lever and quadrant incorporated in the brake unit. The operating lever gives movement to valves through the medium of a compression spring so arranged that the amount of steam brake application is proportional to the compression of the spring, full application of the brake is obtained when this lever is placed in the last notch, the spring box then being solid.

The brake arrangement which was fitted to the former L.M.S. standard locomotives is very similar to the B.R. standard, except for the Driver's brake application valve, which is shown in Fig. 67. This is a combined steam and vacuum brake application valve and is designed to admit steam to the brake cylinders as the train pipe vacuum is reduced and to release steam from the steam brake cylinders as the vacuum is restored. The normal or "off" position is when the small ejector is in operation and a vacuum is maintained in the train pipe and on the inner side of the air piston, the opposite side of the air piston being under atmospheric pressure entering through the hollow piston rod, the air pressure holding the piston in the "in" position which, through the fulcrum lever, maintains the steam brake supply plug in the closed position and at the same time allows the exhaust passage and ports to be in communication with the pipe to the steam brake cylinders.

A movement of the application valve handle to the "on" position admits air into the train pipe through the holes in the application valve disc and to the inner side of the air piston, the air piston then being in equilibrium, the steam behind the steam plug exerts a pressure, forcing the steam plug out. The movement of the steam plug spindle closes the passage and ports, preventing the steam

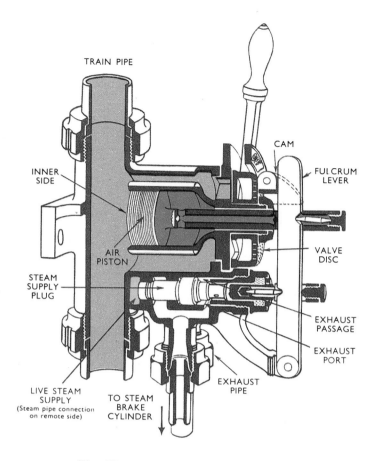

TRAIN PIPE

CAM

INNER SIDE

FULCRUM LEVER

AIR PISTON

VALVE DISC

STEAM SUPPLY PLUG

EXHAUST PASSAGE

EXHAUST PORT

LIVE STEAM SUPPLY
(Steam pipe connection on remote side)

TO STEAM BRAKE CYLINDER

EXHAUST PIPE

Fig. 67   DRIVER'S BRAKE VALVE

passing out to exhaust and at the same time, through the fulcrum lever, forces the air piston out. Steam from the plug passes down the steam pipe to the engine and tender steam brake cylinders. A cam, which is part of the application valve disc, ensures the positive movement of the lever to open the steam plug as the vacuum is being destroyed.

Replacing the application valve to "off" position, the vacuum will be restored in the train pipe and inner side of the air piston. The atmospheric pressure acting on the outer side of the air piston will exert a pressure to force the piston in and through the fulcrum lever, close the steam plug, and allow the steam in the steam brake

Fig. 68   BRAKE ARRANGEMENT ON ENGINE AND TENDER

Former Great Western Railway

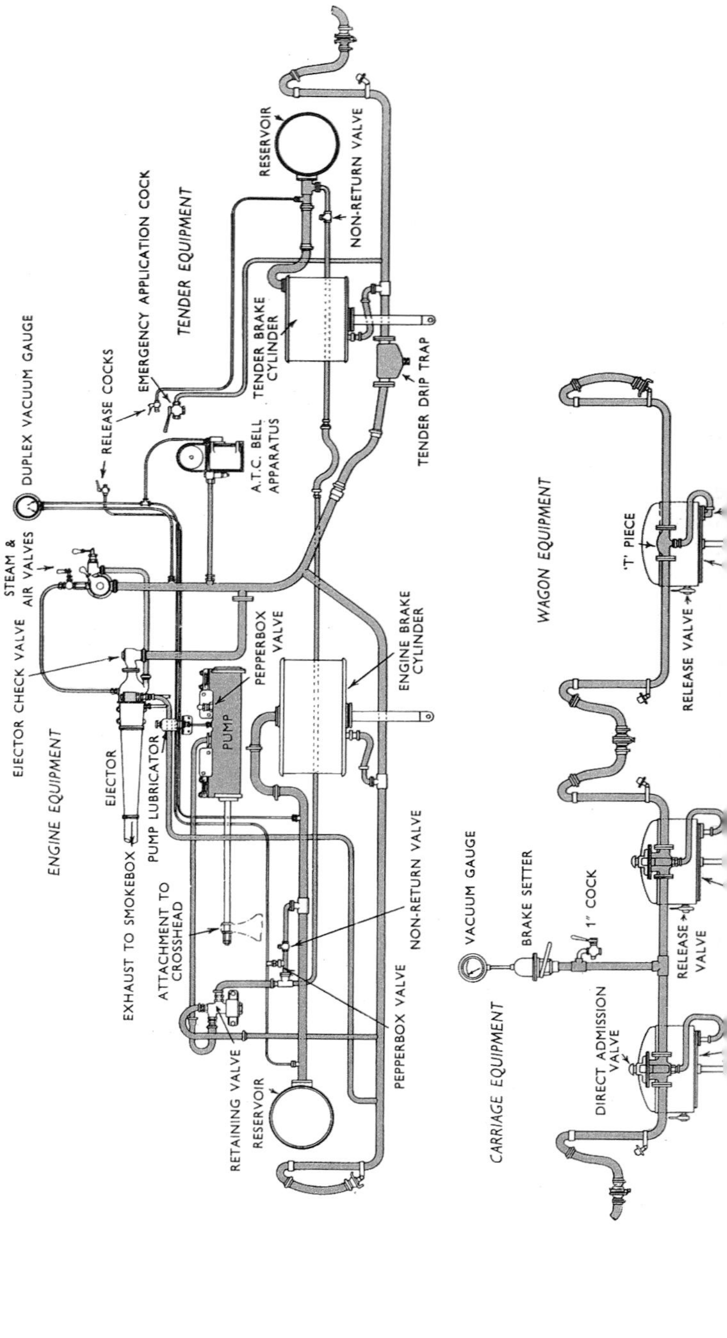

Fig. 68

cylinders to escape to exhaust. For use when the engine is standing, a hook is provided to hold the fulcrum lever in the inward position, ensuring steam plug being held closed, avoiding the need for using the small ejector and resulting in a saving of steam.

Fig. 68 illustrates a brake arrangement which is in common use on the large former G.W.R. locomotives. In this arrangement the engine and tender, in addition to the train, are provided with vacuum brakes. The arrangement is very similar to that previously described.

The four-cone ejector is located on the right-hand side of the boiler outside the cab. The steam to the ejectors is provided from steam valves located on the Driver's brake application valve. The main ejector steam valve supplies steam to the three cones and the small valve supplies steam to the remaining single cone. The vacuum pump is provided to maintain the vacuum when running, and this is supplemented as necessary by the single-cone ejector (small ejector). The three-cone ejector (large ejector) is coupled to the train pipe extension to the Driver's brake application valve through the check valves. The single-cone ejector (small ejector) and the pump are coupled to the train pipe at the front end of the locomotive, the latter by way of the retaining valve. The arrangement of these pipes is the result of protracted experiments to obviate the possibility of water which might accumulate in the flexible train pipe connections through condensation caused by the admission of air into the train pipe during cold or wet weather. The action of the small cone ejector and pump tends to draw any moisture towards the front end of the train pipe on the locomotive, thus keeping the moisture away from the flexible coupling of the train pipe.

The vacuum pump (Fig. 69) consists of a piston which reciprocates

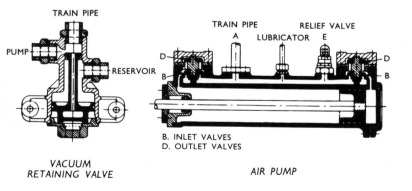

Fig. 69 VACUUM PUMP
Former Great Western Railway Locomotives

in the cylinder, being driven directly from one of the locomotive piston crossheads. A chamber extends above the cylinder and flat clack valves (B) are fitted between the chamber and the cylinder, one at each end. Similar flat clacks (D) are also fitted at each end of the cylinders which lift to provide access to the atmosphere. Train pipe (A) provides communication to the retaining valve.

As the piston travels from the left-hand cover air is induced from the chamber and pipe (A), past clack (B), clack (D) being held on its seating by the pressure of the outside atmosphere. On the return stroke the air previously induced into the cylinder is expelled from the cylinder past clack (D) into the atmosphere, valve (B) being held on its seating by the air being expelled. The pump is double acting so that when air is being induced from the train pipe on one side of the piston, the air induced during the previous stroke is being expelled at the other side.

The retaining valve is shown in Fig. 70. Position 1 shows the

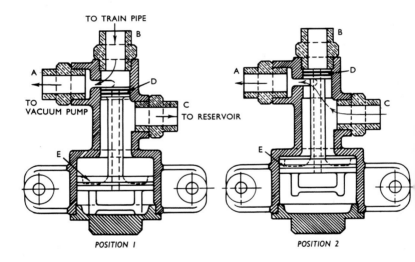

Fig. 70 RETAINING VALVE
Former G.W.R. Locomotives

valve connected at (A) to the pump and (B) to the train pipe and at (C) to the vacuum reservoir. There will thus be always the same amount of vacuum above the small piston (D) and also the large piston (E) as in the train pipe, as the two pistons are connected by means of a hole through the piston rod. In the space between the piston heads there will be the same amount of vacuum as in the reservoir. When running, air is extracted from the train pipe by the vacuum pump.

When the brake is applied air enters the train pipe and then flows underneath the large piston (E) and raises the pistons to the position shown in *Position* 2. It will be noted that the piston (D) seals the passage (B) and being raised above the passage (A) opens communication between the latter and the passage (C), and the effect of the pump being transferred to maintaining the vacuum in the reservoir.

The vacuum relief valve or pepper-box valve on the connecting pipe prevents the vacuum in the reservoir from rising to an excessive amount and preventing the brake pistons from returning to their normal position when the brake is released. The relief valve is set to lift at 23 in. vacuum.

Returning to Fig. 68, when the brake is applied air is admitted to the train pipe and from there to the undersides of the brake pistons on the engine, tender and train. This action of the retaining valve transfers the effect of the pump to the reservoir side of the brake cylinders, therefore maintaining the reservoir vacuum.

When the brake is released the single-cone ejector should be used, whereas the three-cone ejector (large ejector) should only be used when it is necessary to create the vacuum quickly. By avoiding the use of the three-cone ejectors a considerable amount of steam will be saved.

Another brake arrangement in common use is shown in Fig. 71.

A combined ejector and Driver's brake application valve is fitted; this may be of the Dreadnought or solid jet type. (Fig. 72.)

A diagrammatic view of the Dreadnought type of combined ejector and brake valve is shown in Fig. 73.

The diagram illustrates the ejector in the "brake off" position, i.e. the brakes are being released, the cam on the main shaft being raised to open the large ejector steam valve and admit steam to the large ejector. At the same time steam passes to the small cone through the small ejector steam valve. This valve should be set by hand so as to withdraw and reduce the steam pressure to about 120 lb., which is the pressure at which this cone is designed to give its greatest efficiency.

Under the influence of both cones air is drawn rapidly from the train pipe past the large ejector air clack, the small ejector air clack, main air clack, and through cavity (D) in the air disc by way of ports (C and B), these ports being in full register in this position of the handle. At the same time air is drawn from the vacuum chambers on engine and tender past release valve.

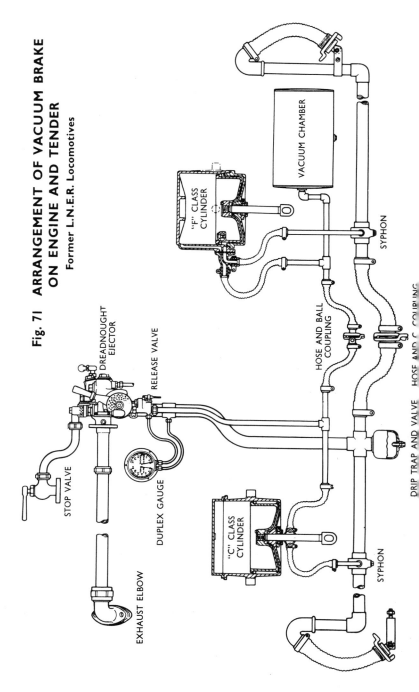

Fig. 71 ARRANGEMENT OF VACUUM BRAKE ON ENGINE AND TENDER

Former L.N.E.R. Locomotives

VACUUM CHAMBER

"F" CLASS CYLINDER

SYPHON

DREADNOUGHT EJECTOR

RELEASE VALVE

HOSE AND BALL COUPLING

STOP VALVE

DUPLEX GAUGE

"C" CLASS CYLINDER

SYPHON

EXHAUST ELBOW

DRIP TRAP AND VALVE   HOSE AND C COUPLING

Fig. 71

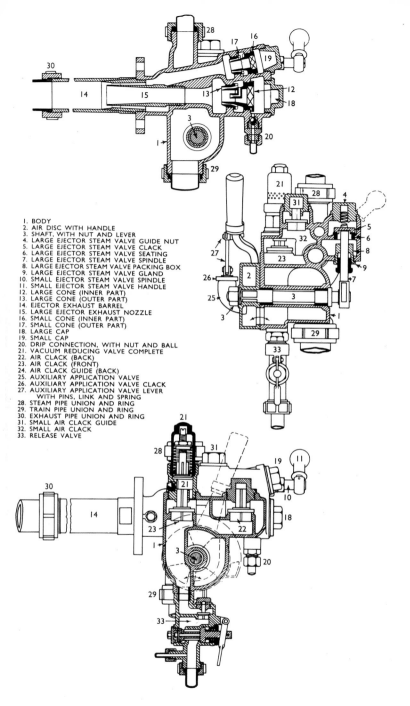

1. BODY
2. AIR DISC WITH HANDLE
3. SHAFT, WITH NUT AND LEVER
4. LARGE EJECTOR STEAM VALVE GUIDE NUT
5. LARGE EJECTOR STEAM VALVE CLACK
6. LARGE EJECTOR STEAM VALVE SEATING
7. LARGE EJECTOR STEAM VALVE SPINDLE
8. LARGE EJECTOR STEAM VALVE PACKING BOX
9. LARGE EJECTOR STEAM VALVE GLAND
10. SMALL EJECTOR STEAM VALVE SPINDLE
11. SMALL EJECTOR STEAM VALVE HANDLE
12. LARGE CONE (INNER PART)
13. LARGE CONE (OUTER PART)
14. EJECTOR EXHAUST BARREL
15. LARGE EJECTOR EXHAUST NOZZLE
16. SMALL CONE (INNER PART)
17. SMALL CONE (OUTER PART)
18. LARGE CAP
19. SMALL CAP
20. DRIP CONNECTION, WITH NUT AND BALL
21. VACUUM REDUCING VALVE COMPLETE
22. AIR CLACK (BACK)
23. AIR CLACK (FRONT)
24. AIR CLACK GUIDE (BACK)
25. AUXILIARY APPLICATION VALVE
26. AUXILIARY APPLICATION VALVE CLACK
27. AUXILIARY APPLICATION VALVE LEVER
    WITH PINS, LINK AND SPRING
28. STEAM PIPE UNION AND RING
29. TRAIN PIPE UNION AND RING
30. EXHAUST PIPE UNION AND RING
31. SMALL AIR CLACK GUIDE
32. SMALL AIR CLACK
33. RELEASE VALVE

Fig. 72 DREADNOUGHT EJECTOR

156

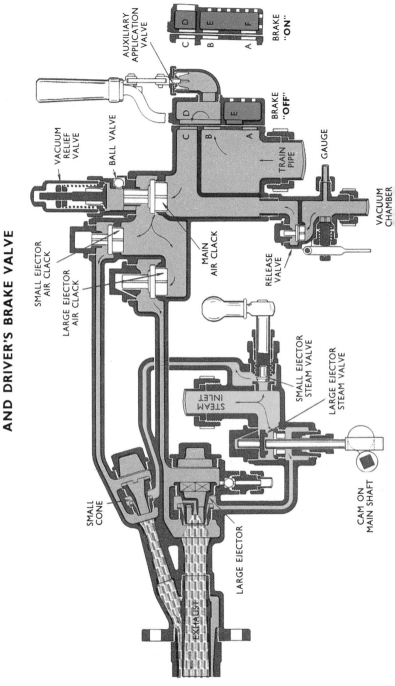

Fig. 73 WORKING DIAGRAM OF DREADNOUGHT VACUUM EJECTOR AND DRIVER'S BRAKE VALVE

AUXILIARY APPLICATION VALVE

BRAKE "ON"

VACUUM RELIEF VALVE

BALL VALVE

BRAKE "OFF"

TRAIN PIPE

GAUGE

VACUUM CHAMBER

SMALL EJECTOR AIR CLACK

LARGE EJECTOR AIR CLACK

MAIN AIR CLACK

RELEASE VALVE

SMALL EJECTOR STEAM VALVE

LARGE EJECTOR STEAM VALVE

STEAM INLET

SMALL CONE

LARGE EJECTOR

CAM ON MAIN SHAFT

EXHAUST

Fig. 73

In the "running position" of handle, the cam lowers the large ejector steam valve on to its seat, thus cutting off the supply of steam to the large ejector. The connection between the small cone and the train pipe through cavity (D) in the air disc remains open and the small ejector maintains the working vacuum whilst the train is running. Operation of the auxiliary application valve in this position admits air to the train pipe and enables light brake applications to be made for controlling the train speed.

As the handle is moved towards the "brake on" position the connection through the cavity (D) is progressively closed. At the same time ports (E and F) in the air disc gradually uncover ports (B and A) in the ejector face and air is admitted to the train pipe to apply the brake. This air is prevented from passing to the engine and tender vacuum chambers by the non-return valve in release valve.

In the full "brake on" position ports (A and B) in the ejector face are completely open to atmosphere through ports (F and E) in the disc and the brake is rapidly applied. At the same time the small cone is isolated from the train pipe by the wall of cavity (D) and draws only on the engine and tender vacuum chambers past the release valve. In this way the maximum possible locomotive brake power is assured in emergency applications.

The air passages in the ejector are so arranged that, in all cases, air from the train pipe is drawn past two gunmetal clacks before coming in contact with the steam. When steam is cut off from the cones and a vacuum is left in the train pipe, these clacks prevent moisture, and more especially smokebox gases, being drawn into the train pipe.

The ball valve, located below the relief valve, communicates with the chamber between the two ejector clacks and the main clack. When a vacuum is created in the instrument the ball is drawn to its seat, but falls off as soon as steam is shut off and the vacuum drops. Should ejector air clacks be leaking it provides an outlet for any vapour or steam. Should the main air clack leak, it admits air from the atmosphere being drawn into the train pipe and so prevents any tendency to draw vapour and smokebox gases through ejector air clacks.

The vacuum relief valve is a spring-loaded valve which limits the degree of vacuum carried in the train pipe. When the point is reached at which it is set, atmospheric pressure above the valve overcomes the resistance in the spring and the valve opens to admit air to the space above the main clack, thus preventing the creation of a higher vacuum in the train pipe.

The release valve enables atmosphere to be admitted direct to the vacuum chambers so that the brake can be released by hand

Fig. 74 WORKING DIAGRAM OF S.J. VACUUM EJECTOR AND DRIVER'S BRAKE VALVE

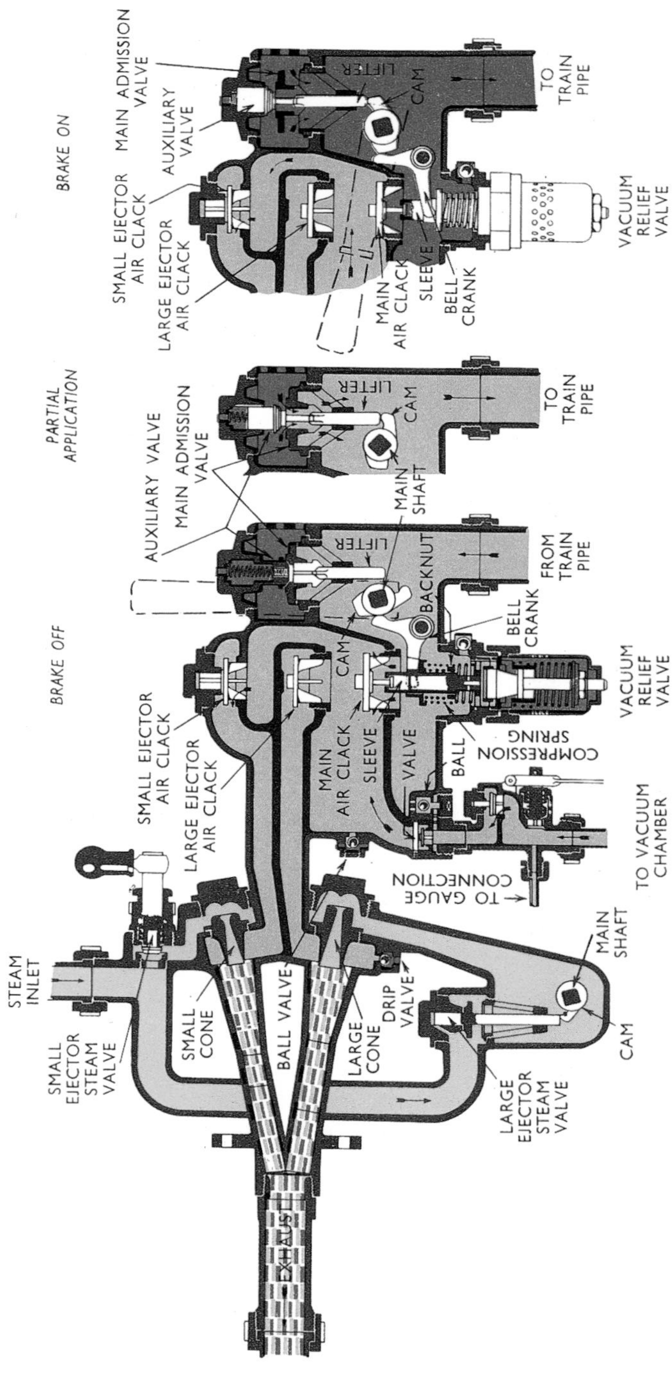

Fig. 74

when the locomotive is uncoupled and when steam is not available.

Fig. 74 shows a diagrammatic arrangement of the solid jet type combined ejector and brake valve.

The left-hand illustration is of the ejector in "brake off" position, the cam on the main shaft being raised to open the large ejector steam valve and admits steam to the large cone. At the same time steam passes to the small cone through the small ejector steam valve which is opened just sufficiently to admit the quantity of steam necessary to maintain the required vacuum.

Under the influence of both cones air is drawn rapidly from the train pipe past the air clacks, also from the chambers on the engine past the valve and the ball.

In the "running position" of the Driver's handle, the cam lowers the large steam valve on to its seat and the working vacuum is maintained throughout the running train by the small cone only, which is prevented from drawing back on the exhaust branch of the large ejector by air clack closing down.

The "partial application" shows the first admission of air as the Driver's handle is moved towards the "brake on" position. The finger on cam engages the lifter to open an auxiliary valve, and after this valve has attained its full lift the shoulders on the wing of the lifter come in contact with the main admission valve.

To effect isolation of the main train pipe from the action of the small ejector in the full "brake on" position, the main air clack is provided with a spindle extension actuated by the sleeve. Bell crank, worked from the cam, is operated increasingly as the Driver's handle comes to the "full on" position. In the "full on" position illustrated the arm of the bell crank has fully depressed the sleeve, taking with it the main clack, so shutting off the small ejector connection from the train pipe. The actual holding down of the main air clack is through the compression spring, which is capable of adjustment as regards tension by means of the backnut. The light spring only serves the purpose of holding this assembly together to prevent chatter.

When the brake is applied and the small ejector is left drawing upon the cavity below the small air clack, the large air clack remains closed and the main air clack is held closed by the bell crank, the valve lifts and connects the engine chambers to the ejector. In this way the maximum possible locomotive brake power is assured in emergency applications. To provide against the creation of an excessive vacuum in the top side of the brake cylinders the main air clack is held down by the bell crank through the tension of the compression spring which is so arranged that, when the brake is "full on" and the cavity all round the bell crank and the train pipe is in a state of atmospheric pressure, the creation of anything exceeding 21 in. above the main air clack will cause the atmospheric pressure under it to overcome the resistance of the compression spring and so allow the main air clack to lift, and this acts as an internal relief valve, obtaining its air from the train pipe which is in a state of atmospheric pressure due to the main admission valve being open.

A ball valve is located in the cavity between the two ejector clacks and the main clack, and is drawn to its seat when a vacuum is created, but falls off as soon as steam is shut off and the vacuum drops. Should the small and large air clacks be leaking, it provides an outlet for any vapour or steam. Should the main air clack leak, this ball valve prevents any tendency to draw vapour and smoke box gases through the small and large air clacks. The ball above the relief valve serves to allow any moisture to escape.

For the purpose of maintaining the brake operative on a "dead engine" which requires moving and may have vacuum brake cylinders without ball valves, the ball is provided within the ejector. By this means, when a vacuum is created in the train pipe, air is also drawn from the chambers of the dead engine, thus created in the train pipe; air is also drawn from the chambers of the dead engine, thus creating a vacuum above and below the brake pistons. This necessitates that the Driver's handle on the dead engine ejector is in the "running position".

The vacuum relief valve is a spring-loaded valve which limits the degree of vacuum carried in the train pipe. When the point is reached at which it is set, the atmospheric pressure below the valve overcomes the resistance of the spring and the valve opens to admit air to the space below the main clack, thus preventing the creation of a higher vacuum in the train pipe.

The release valve operates in the usual manner.

Fig. 75 shows the brake arrangement on ex-L.N.E.R. A.3 Pacific locomotives.

The combined ejector and Driver's brake valve is of the combined type and the vacuum brake cylinders are of the combined "C" class without release valve.

On the arrangement Figs. D and A illustrate the normal running position with the brakes "off" and the small ejector maintaining the vacuum in the train pipe and vacuum cylinder. Figs. F and B illustrate the position when the brake is in the "on" position.

It will be noted that air has entered the train pipe through the Driver's control handle and has acted on the underside of the brake cylinders causing the brakes to be applied. The effect of the small ejector has been cut off from the train pipe and its whole effect transferred to maintaining the vacuum in the vacuum chamber on the top side of the brake cylinders so as to overcome any slight leakages which might decrease the vacuum.

Vacuum Brake Cylinders

Figs. 76-79 show four types of vacuum brake cylinder which are in common use on British Railways. Fig. 76 illustrates the combined "C"-type cylinder which is in general use on carriage and wagon stock as no vacuum chamber is required, this being incorporated in the design. The piston is rendered airtight by means of a rubber rolling ring (9).

Fig. 79 illustrates a similar cylinder, but the piston is fitted with a slipping rubber band instead of a rolling ring, and this type was adopted as standard for British Railways stock.

With rolling ring cylinders the vacuum chamber side vacuum is obtained either through a non-return ball valve in the piston or in an external fitting on the cylinder. These allow air to flow from the chamber side and shut when the brake is applied, so as to maintain the vacuum in the vacuum chamber.

The former G.W.R. slipping-band type of brake cylinder does not require ball valves, the air being drawn past the rubber band which, when the piston is right down in the "off" position, lies opposite a relieving groove.

When the brake is applied, air which enters the train pipe through the Driver's brake application valve, or, for that matter, the Guard's brake application valve, passes through the brake cylinder flexible connecting pipe and enters into the bottom of the brake cylinder and at the same time forces the ball valve on to its seating on the passage leading to the vacuum chamber, in the case of the rolling ring cylinder, thereby retaining the vacuum on the top side of the brake piston, the air having access to the bottom of the piston only.

When the brakes are released, the action of the ejector causes air to be drawn from the underside of the brake piston. When the vacuum reaches and commences to exceed that in the vacuum chamber (top side of brake piston) the ball valve lifts from its seating until the vacuum on both sides of the brake piston is the same, and being in equilibrium the brake piston drops to the bottom of the brake cylinder by virtue of its weight.

With the slipping-band cylinder, when the vacuum in the train pipe commences to exceed that in the vacuum chamber, the brake piston drops to the "off" and air from the vacuum chamber is drawn past the rubber band opposite the relieving groove.

Fig. 75 BRAKE ARRANGEME

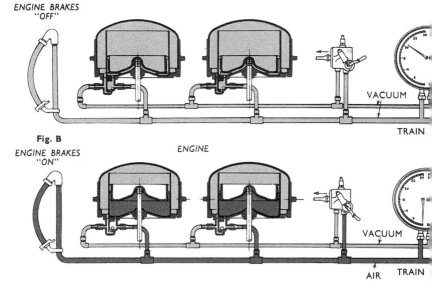

Fig. A
ENGINE BRAKES "OFF"

VACUUM

TRAIN

Fig. B
ENGINE BRAKES "ON"

ENGINE

VACUUM

AIR TRAIN

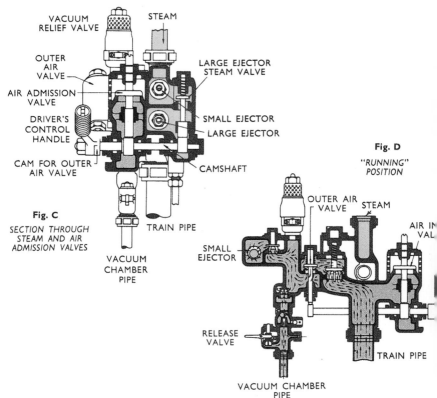

VACUUM RELIEF VALVE

STEAM

OUTER AIR VALVE

LARGE EJECTOR STEAM VALVE

AIR ADMISSION VALVE

DRIVER'S CONTROL HANDLE

SMALL EJECTOR

LARGE EJECTOR

CAM FOR OUTER AIR VALVE

CAMSHAFT

Fig. C
SECTION THROUGH STEAM AND AIR ADMISSION VALVES

TRAIN PIPE

VACUUM CHAMBER PIPE

Fig. D
"RUNNING" POSITION

OUTER AIR VALVE

STEAM

AIR IN VAL

SMALL EJECTOR

RELEASE VALVE

TRAIN PIPE

VACUUM CHAMBER PIPE

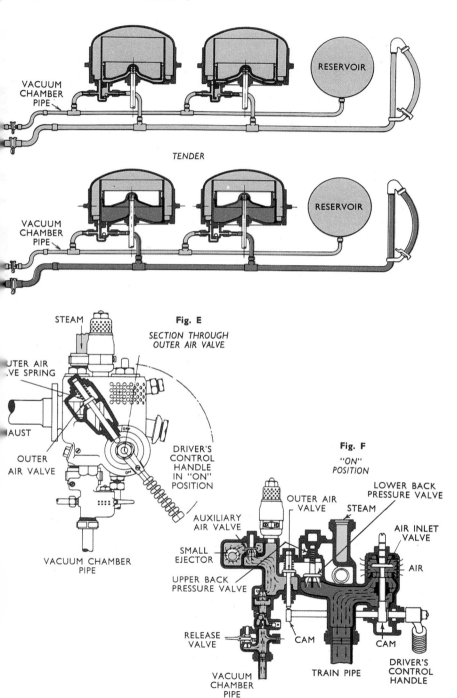

VACUUM
CHAMBER
PIPE

RESERVOIR

TENDER

VACUUM
CHAMBER
PIPE

RESERVOIR

STEAM

Fig. E

*SECTION THROUGH
OUTER AIR VALVE*

UTER AIR
VE SPRING

AUST

OUTER
AIR VALVE

DRIVER'S
CONTROL
HANDLE
IN "ON"
POSITION

Fig. F

*"ON"
POSITION*

LOWER BACK
PRESSURE VALVE

OUTER AIR
VALVE

STEAM

AIR INLET
VALVE

AIR

AUXILIARY
AIR VALVE

SMALL
EJECTOR

UPPER BACK
PRESSURE VALVE

VACUUM CHAMBER
PIPE

RELEASE
VALVE

CAM

CAM

DRIVER'S
CONTROL
HANDLE

VACUUM
CHAMBER
PIPE

TRAIN PIPE

164

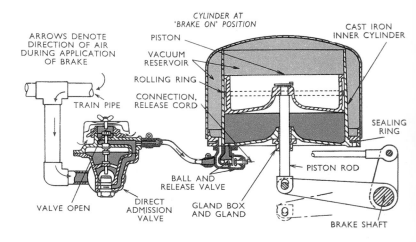

Fig. 76 **VACUUM BRAKE CYLINDER**
C. Class Combined

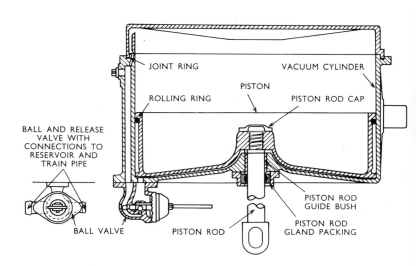

Fig. 78 **VACUUM BRAKE SEPARATE CYLINDER**
C. Class

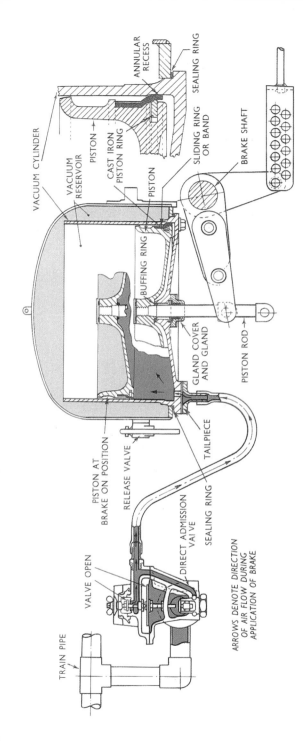

ANNULAR RECESS

SEALING RING

VACUUM CYLINDER

PISTON

VACUUM RESERVOIR

CAST IRON PISTON RING

SLIDING RING OR BAND

BRAKE SHAFT

PISTON

BUFFING RING

PISTON ROD

GLAND COVER AND GLAND

PISTON AT BRAKE ON POSITION

RELEASE VALVE

TAILPIECE

DIRECT ADMISSION VALVE

SEALING RING

VALVE OPEN

TRAIN PIPE

ARROWS DENOTE DIRECTION OF AIR FLOW DURING APPLICATION OF BRAKE

Fig. 77 VACUUM BRAKE CYLINDER (COMBINED) SLIPPING-BAND TYPE

B.R. standard for coaching stock

L

Fig. 77

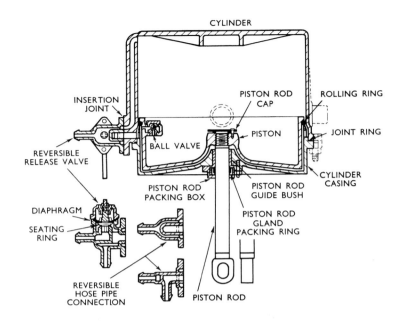

Fig. 79 VACUUM BRAKE SEPARATE CYLINDER
F. Class

The Westinghouse Automatic Air Brake

This is a compressed-air brake and Fig. 80 shows a diagrammatic arrangement of the system as applied to a locomotive.

On a steam locomotive, air is compressed by a steam-driven pump which is automatically controlled by means of a "governor" (see Fig. 81) positioned on the pump steam supply line. The governor is usually set to maintain a pressure of 90 lb. per sq. in. in the main reservoir, which pressure is indicated by the red hand of the duplex air pressure gauge.

The compressed-air supply from the main reservoir passes through the Driver's brake application valve (Fig. 82) into the train pipe by means of the feed valve (Fig. 83) which automatically maintains the air pressure in the train pipe at 70 lb. per sq. in. when the Driver's brake application valve is set in the "running" position.

The brake equipment on the engine, tender and each vehicle of the train fitted with this type of brake is a triple valve, auxiliary air reservoir and brake cylinder.

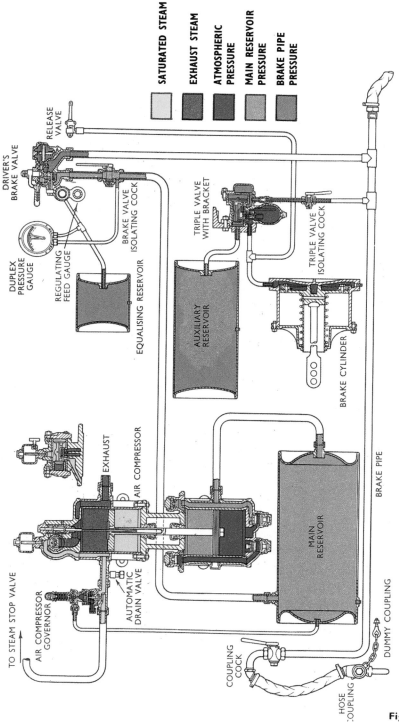

SATURATED STEAM

EXHAUST STEAM

ATMOSPHERIC PRESSURE

MAIN RESERVOIR PRESSURE

BRAKE PIPE PRESSURE

RELEASE VALVE

DRIVER'S BRAKE VALVE

BRAKE VALVE ISOLATING COCK

TRIPLE VALVE WITH BRACKET

TRIPLE VALVE ISOLATING COCK

DUPLEX PRESSURE GAUGE

REGULATING FEED GAUGE

EQUALISING RESERVOIR

AUXILIARY RESERVOIR

BRAKE CYLINDER

EXHAUST

AIR COMPRESSOR

TO STEAM STOP VALVE

AIR COMPRESSOR GOVERNOR

AUTOMATIC DRAIN VALVE

MAIN RESERVOIR

BRAKE PIPE

COUPLING COCK

HOSE COUPLING

DUMMY COUPLING

Fig. 80 DIAGRAM OF WESTINGHOUSE AUTOMATIC BRAKE

Fig. 80

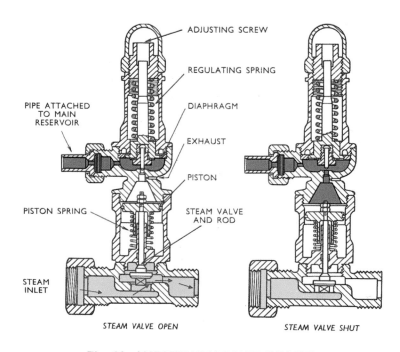

STEAM VALVE OPEN

STEAM VALVE SHUT

Fig. 81 WESTINGHOUSE BRAKE AIR COMPRESSOR GOVERNOR

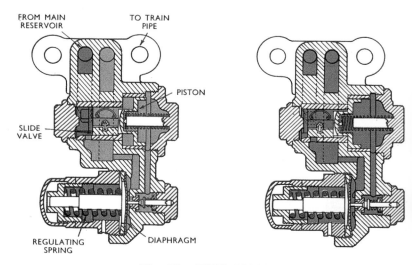

Fig. 83 FEED VALVE

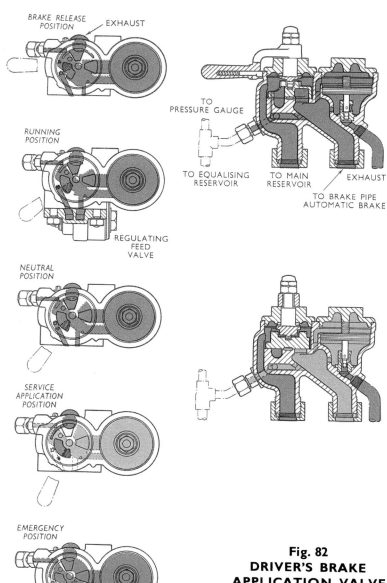

BRAKE RELEASE POSITION

EXHAUST

RUNNING POSITION

REGULATING FEED VALVE

NEUTRAL POSITION

SERVICE APPLICATION POSITION

EMERGENCY POSITION

TO PRESSURE GAUGE

TO EQUALISING RESERVOIR

TO MAIN RESERVOIR

EXHAUST

TO BRAKE PIPE AUTOMATIC BRAKE

Fig. 82
DRIVER'S BRAKE
APPLICATION VALVE

The triple valve (Fig. 84), as the name implies, has three duties to perform: (1) charging the auxiliary reservoirs, (2) applying the brakes, and (3) releasing the brakes.

When the locomotive is coupled to the train, air is admitted to the train pipe after the cocks between the locomotive (tender) and the train have been opened. Driver's brake application valve handle is then placed in the "release" position (see Fig. 82) until the black hand of the duplex air gauge indicates that the normal train pipe working pressure has been reached, after which the brake valve handle should then be placed in the "running" position.

The air in the train pipe passes into each triple valve (see Fig. 84) and forces up the piston which is connected to a slide valve. In this position compressed air from the train pipe charges the auxiliary reservoirs through the grooves until the air pressure equals that in the train pipe, at the same time the slide valve establishes communication between the brake cylinder and exhaust passage through the cavity.

When the brake is applied the air pressure in the train pipe is reduced and the piston is moved downwards by the greater air pressure in the auxiliary reservoir. The piston, having a limited movement, without acting on the slide valve, closes the feed groove and at the same time moves the graduating valve from its seating, thus opening the port. Further downward movement of the piston takes with it the slide valve which closes the exhaust passage and brings the port into communication with the passage to the brake cylinder, resulting in air entering the brake cylinder from the auxiliary reservoir and the brakes being applied. Further downward movement of the piston and the slide valve is arrested with the decrease of pressure above the piston, i.e. in the auxiliary reservoir, due to the flow of air to the brake cylinder, and when the pressure in the auxiliary reservoir is reduced slightly below that in the train pipe, the piston moves up sufficiently to close the graduating valve (but not sufficient to move the slide valve). By further reducing the train pipe pressure any degree of brake pressure can be attained. The brakes are fully applied, however, when the train pipe pressure has been reduced by 25 lb. per sq. in., and any further reduction, under normal braking conditions, is merely a waste of compressed air.

When an emergency application of the brake is made, the piston is forced downwards to the limit of its stroke and seats on the leather gasket. When this occurs, the slide valve uncovers fully the passage to the brake cylinder, thus allowing the air from the auxiliary reservoir to enter quickly the brake cylinder and apply the brakes with full force.

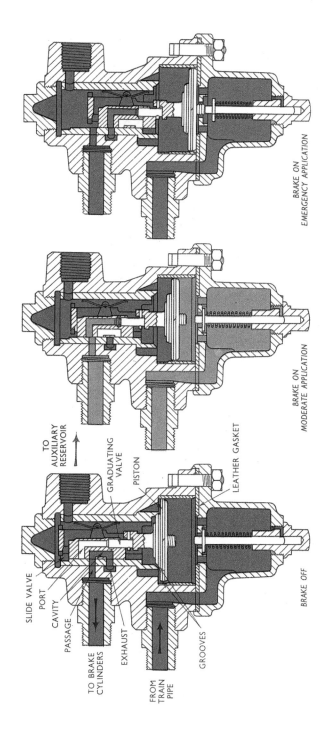

Fig. 84 TRIPLE VALVE (Ordinary)

Fig. 84

When trains are worked with two locomotives, the brakes should be entirely under the control of the Driver of the leading engine. On the train engine the isolating cock to the main reservoir pipe under the Driver's brake application valve must be closed and the brake valve placed in the "release" position. Care should be taken to ensure that this isolating cock is opened on the train engine whenever the leading engine is uncoupled.

If the train should become divided, or a flexible coupling burst, the brakes will be automatically applied on both portions of the train owing to the reduction in train pipe pressure. The Driver, under these circumstances, should move his brake application valve to the "on" position, as when making an ordinary application. This will prevent the air escaping from the main reservoir and assist the stopping.

The same applies when the brake is applied by the cock in the guard's van being opened.

The improved triple valve is shown in Fig. 85; its object is to give a closer approach to simultaneous action of all the triple valves on a train when the slide valve is moved by applying the brakes, the bulb is closed to atmosphere and opened to the train pipe. The local reduction of the train pipe pressure thereby produced by the forward triple valves of a train causes an earlier action of the rearward triple valves, which results in a more nearly simultaneous braking effect being produced throughout the train in every case of first setting the brakes than was possible with the ordinary triple valve.

The bulb at the bottom of the valve is made in different sizes proportioned to the volume of the vehicle train pipe.

To release the brakes, air from the main reservoir is admitted by means of the Driver's valve into the main brake pipe where it enters the triple valve and forces piston and slide valve to their original position; the air from the brake cylinders of bulb is then discharged to atmosphere and the brakes released. The auxiliary reservoir is then recharged through the grooves, past the piston, as in the case of the ordinary triple valve.

Fig. 86 illustrates the brake arrangement of a dual-fitted locomotive; whilst the brakes on the engine are Westinghouse, it is possible to work coaches equipped with vacuum brakes. This is done by means of a proportional valve, which ensures that the degree of application and release of the brakes on the engine and train are in proportion to each other.

Westinghouse Brake Cylinder

The brake cylinder consists of a piston and piston rod which are attached to the brake gear in such a manner that the brake blocks

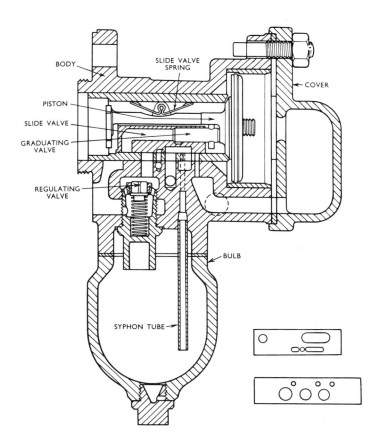

Fig. 85 TRIPLE VALVE (Improved)

are pressed against the wheels when the piston is moved in the brake cylinder by air pressure. A spring is fitted which is compressed when the brake is applied, and when the brake is released the spring expands and returns the piston and brake gear to their original position, thus releasing the brake blocks from the wheels.

To prevent the application of the brakes, which might be caused by a slight leakage in the brake pipe to the brake cylinder, the brake cylinders are provided with a small groove which establishes communication between both sides of the piston when the brake piston is in the "off" position. If a slight leakage occurs the air will

174

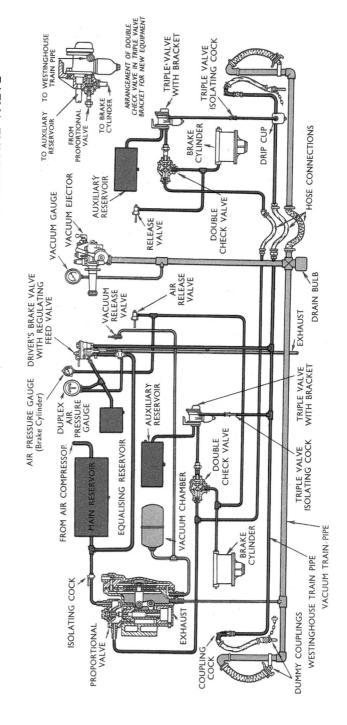

Fig. 86 WESTINGHOUSE BRAKE DIAGRAM
AUTOMATIC BRAKE ON ENGINE AND TENDER WITH PROPORTIONAL VALVE

Fig. 86

pass through the groove to the atmosphere without moving the piston. However, when a considerable quantity of air is admitted to the cylinder, as by an ordinary brake application, the piston is immediately forced past the groove and the escape of air sealed.

Questions and Answers

(1) *Q.* How is the train pipe vacuum measured?

A. The vacuum is measured in "inches of mercury" and the vacuum gauges on the engine and in the brake vans are graduated in inches. A perfect vacuum corresponds to approximately 30 in. of mercury, atmospheric pressure or no vacuum to zero inches. The regulation of vacuum in the train pipe to 21 in. of mercury, which it is important to bear in mind, along with other intermediate readings, is only a partial vacuum. Each 1 lb. pressure of air extracted is represented by 2 in. of vacuum on the gauge.

(2) *Q.* What will be the pressure per square inch on the piston when the brake is applied fully if 21 in. of vacuum is recorded on the gauge before the application is made?

A. $10\frac{1}{2}$ lb. per sq. in. Atmospheric pressure or the weight of air pressing upon the earth's surface is approximately 15 lb. per sq. in. at sea level and it has been found that this pressure is sufficient to support a column of mercury nearly 30 in. high. Consequently every inch of mercury in the column represents a pressure of $\frac{1}{2}$ lb. per sq. in., so that 21 in. indicated in the vacuum gauge represents $10\frac{1}{2}$ lb. per sq. in. which can be exerted upon the piston head when the brake is applied. Some idea of the power available can be obtained by considering a 20-in. diameter cylinder. The area of the piston is 314 sq. in. and the pull produced on the brake piston rod would be $10\frac{1}{2} \times 314$ lb., which equals 3,297 lb. or more than 1 ton.

(3) *Q.* How does the combination ejector create vacuum?

A. A jet of steam issuing at high velocity from a cone of special shape within the ejector (see Fig. 64) carries the surrounding air forward by frictional contact through a second and larger cone, known as the air cone, to exhaust in the smokebox.

The removal of air in this manner from the space in the immediate vicinity of the steam jet sets up a partial vacuum inside the ejector; air, in its endeavour to fill this space, flows past the non-return valve from the train pipe and other portions of the brake apparatus connected to it.

In this way it is possible to maintain the desired amount of vacuum at will in the train pipe and connections so long as the ejector is kept at work and the brake is not applied. The combination ejector contains two separate ejectors constructed on the above principle, each one independent of the other and possessing its own non-return valves.

(4) *Q*. What purpose do the non-return valves serve?

A. The non-return valves and the air lock chamber are for the purpose of preventing loss of vacuum through the ejector cones when the ejector is shut down, and also to guard against steam and smokebox gases being allowed to enter the train pipe and connections.

(5) *Q*. How is the train pipe vacuum prevented from rising above the regulation amount of 21 in.?

A. A vacuum relief valve is provided for the purpose. This is a spring-loaded valve capable of being adjusted so that it will open and admit air to the train pipe as soon as the regulation vacuum of 21 in. has been exceeded. The relief valve is generally mounted inside the cab in an accessible position and contains a fine-gauge filter to prevent entry of dust and dirt into the train pipe. This filter requires to be cleaned and examined periodically by the Shed Staff. If the filter or the air holes become choked with dirt or any other obstruction, free passage of air to the relief valve is prevented and may result in an excessive amount of vacuum being created in the train pipe.

(6) *Q*. Describe one type of vacuum brake cylinder in common use.

A. A type of vacuum brake cylinder frequently used on passenger and freight vehicles is illustrated in Fig. 76.

It will be seen to consist of a vacuum reservoir and cylinder combined, the cylinder proper being open at the top and enclosed within the reservoir. The brake piston is of fairly deep section and is kept airtight within the cylinder by a rubber rolling ring nipped between the piston head and the cylinder wall. The piston rod passes through the bottom of the cylinder and is kept airtight by a gland.

The brake cylinder is connected to the train pipe by a small flexible hose attached to the ball valve housing at the base of the vacuum chamber.

The purpose of this ball valve is to control the movement

of the brake piston in accordance with the variations in the train pipe vacuum, and also to provide a means of releasing the brake by hand when necessary.

This ball valve can close the vacuum chamber port, or it can place the lower side of the brake piston and the vacuum chamber in communication with each other and with the train pipe when off its seating.

Running with the brake off, the ball valve is unseated, leaving the train pipe in communication with both sides of the piston, which will then be in equilibrium and resting by its own weight at the bottom of the cylinder. Immediately air is admitted to the train pipe it passes up the connecting pipe and forces the ball valve to its seating on the port leading to the vacuum chamber, thereby retaining the vacuum on the top side of the piston. The port to the underside of the piston is, however, left open, and the air accordingly flows into the bottom of the cylinder, lifts the piston and applies the brake.

Restoration of the train pipe vacuum extracts the air from below the piston until the vacuum below equals that in the chamber above, after which the piston, being equalised, will sink to the bottom of the cylinder by its own weight, allowing the brake to release. At the same time the ball valve will drop away from its seating on the chamber port, leaving both sides of the piston in communication with the train pipe, ready for the next brake application.

The hand release arrangement is effected by a ball valve enclosed inside a sliding cage connected to an external lever, as shown in Fig. 76. When the release cord is pulled, the cage is displaced, forcing the ball valve away from the vacuum chamber port, thereby placing both sides of the brake piston in communication with the train pipe.

(7) *Q.* Passenger vehicles are fitted with a communication cord which, when operated, gives an indication to the Driver in order to stop the train in case of emergency. Describe how the arrangement operates.

    A. The communication cord consists of a chain passing through each compartment of the coach and connected at the end of the vehicle to the passengers' alarm valve and indicating disc.

The alarm valve, when operated by the chain being pulled, opens and allows air to enter the vacuum train pipe, causing a reduction in vacuum of 5 to 10 in., which is sufficient to apply the brake with moderate force and to attract the Driver's attention.

(8) *Q*. Describe the brake action on a train fitted throughout with the vacuum automatic brake.

   A. The brake is applied by the pressure of air being admitted through the ports of the Driver's application valve, passing down the train pipe from the engine to the train.

   During release, the blocks on the leading vehicles will be freed first and for this reason the small ejector only should be used for release purposes when the train is in motion, in order to avoid surging and shocks on the drawgear caused by the early release in front and continued retardation of the rear portion of the train, which would be intensified if the large ejector was used.

(9) *Q*. How should the brake be handled to obtain the best results?

   A. In the case of "service application", in which full brake power is not called for, the Driver should begin by destroying 7 to 10 in. of train pipe vacuum and should hold this application until he feels the slight check which will indicate the brake has taken hold. This is known as "setting the brake"; after this, the brake block pressure can be varied at will by regulating the train pipe vacuum to suit requirements of the stop.

   To make a full-power application, the Driver would put the application valve right over to "full on" position in a single movement, destroying all train pipe vacuum, and would leave it thus until speed was reduced sufficiently to permit the application to be somewhat eased.

(10) *Q*. Name a few bad faults to be avoided when handling vacuum-fitted trains.

   A. Do not "see-saw" the brake handle between "running" and "brake on" positions several times when commencing an application. This practice retards the action of the brake cylinder ball valves and will increase the time required to "set" the brake.

   In all normal cases avoid the use of the large ejector to release the brake except when the train is stationary.

   Do not bring the train to rest with all the train pipe vacuum destroyed and the brake applied with full power.

   Ease the application in the final stages by allowing the train pipe vacuum to build up slowly to about 12 in., which will prevent complete release of the engine brake and also the risk of locked wheels on the train.

(11) *Q.* How would the Driver carry out his test of the brake on an engine fitted with the automatic steam and vacuum brake?

A. He would test for obstruction in the engine train pipe by applying the large ejector with first the front and then the rear hose bag off the stopper; in neither case should the vacuum gauge show more than 3 in. of vacuum. If the gauge shows an appreciable amount of vacuum with either pipe off the plug, an obstruction in the train pipe is indicated and must be located and removed. Having replaced the hosebags on the stoppers he should then create the full 21 in. of vacuum in the train pipe, using the small ejector for the purpose; shut off the ejector and note the time taken for the vacuum to fall to 12 in. on the gauge.

If this is less than 20 seconds the train pipe leakage is excessive and should be located.

The large ejector should be tested and the brake worked once or twice by the application valve to prove the mechanical parts of the apparatus.

(12) *Q.* If bad leakage on the train pipe is indicated by this test, what points should be looked at to find the fault?

A. See that both vacuum hose pipes are properly on the stop plugs and that the rubber washers are good. Test the drip valves for leakage and all joints in the train pipe, using the torch-light flame for the purpose. See that the disc of the application valve is not sticking away from the face and check all the train pipe connections on the footplate. If no leakages are disclosed, suspect the non-return valves in the combination ejector. Whilst making the above test the small ejector should be kept at work and the brake valve should be left in "running" position.

(13) *Q.* How would you test engines fitted with the vacuum brake before leaving the shed?

A. Examine the flexible train pipes and see that the couplings fit properly on the plugs. Then put the brake handle to the "on" position, close the auxiliary release valve and open the small ejector steam valve slightly. This will extract air from the top sides of the pistons and admit air to the bottom sides and train pipe and will also deposit in the smokebox any water which may be in the exhaust pipe instead of throwing it out over the boiler, as may be the case if the large ejector was suddenly opened after the engine had been standing for some time. Close the small ejector and watch the chamber side needle on the gauge, which will fall if the ball valve leaks. If the needle remains stationary, then test the train pipe side by creating 21 in. with the application valve in "running" position, close the steam valve and watch the gauge. If the vacuum is rapidly destroyed, the defect must be located and made good.

The large ejector must be tested separately, preferably outside the shed, whilst the small ejector remains shut. Then test the train pipe on the engine by taking first the front hosepipe and afterwards the rear hosepipe off the plugs separately, and opening the large ejector fully and then closing it; if any vacuum is registered on the train pipe side of the gauge when the ejector is closed whilst either of the hosepipes is off the plug, a stoppage or obstruction in the train pipe is indicated, which must be put right.

(14) *Q.* On engines fitted with vacuum brake only, how would you decide if a chamber-side leakage was internal or external?

A. Create a vacuum on both sides, close the small ejector and leave the application valve in "running" position. If the chamber-side pointer should fall it will be an external leakage.

(15) *Q.* How would you test for a faulty ball valve, burst diaphragm or faulty rolling ring?

A. Create 21 in., close the small ejector and apply the brake quickly, returning the application valve into "running" position. A fault will be shown by the chamber-side needle falling and the train pipe needle rising until equal.

(16) *Q.* Is it possible to have a defect without indication on the engine vacuum gauge?

A. Yes, an obstruction in the train pipe might prevent the creation of vacuum in the train, but the engine gauge would show the correct amount of vacuum. It would be necessary to test the engine with the vacuum hosepipe off the plug, as previously explained. (It should be borne in mind that the vacuum gauge shows the degree of vacuum but can give no indication of the quantity of air the ejector can eject to overcome leakage. The small ejector may maintain 21 in. of vacuum on the engine alone, but when coupled to the train is unable to create or maintain the requisite vacuum. The test for this is by the use of a disc with a standard size leak-hole; this is carried out by the Fitting staff at the shed or by C. & W. staff when in traffic. See General Appendix and Supplement "Working of Vacuum Brake".)

(17) *Q*. How should the brake be operated when two engines, coupled together, are attached to a vacuum-fitted train?

A. It is the duty of the Driver of the leading engine to create and maintain the vacuum and to operate the brake. The ejectors on the second engine must be kept closed, but the Driver of the second engine is not relieved from responsibility of the due observance of all signals affecting the working of the train and in case of need he must apply the brake.

(18) *Q*. How does the compressed air used in the Westinghouse brake system apply the brake?

A. By the air being admitted to a brake cylinder and forcing the piston out, which by means of connecting rods and levers forces the brake blocks against the wheels.

(19) *Q*. What essential parts of the brake are fitted to engine and tender carriage or other vehicle?

A. An auxiliary reservoir, triple valve and brake cylinder.

(20) *Q*. Where is the pressure which supplies the brake cylinder stored?

A. In the auxiliary reservoir under each vehicle fitted with the brake.

(21) *Q*. How much main reservoir pressure should be carried?

A. 90 lb. per sq. in.

SECTION 9

AUTOMATIC TRAIN CONTROL

Automatic train control is the name given to the various systems which give an audible and, in some cases, a visual indication in the engine cab of the position of a distant signal, followed by a brake application where necessary. There are three systems in operation in this country:—

(a) The former Great Western Railway system in use on the Western Region (Fig. 87).

(b) The system in use on the Eastern Region (London, Tilbury and Southend section) (Fig. 88).

(c) The British Railways system (Fig. 89).

The B.R. system which has been developed during the past five years will be adopted as the standard for use on all British Railways.

The methods of operation of the three systems are described in the following pages, but it may be helpful to outline the main features of each arrangement.

Former Great Western Railway System

In this system a fixed ramp about 44 ft. long is situated in the 4-ft. way. This makes contact with a shoe on the locomotive, and when the distant signal is at Caution the ramp lifts the shoe operating a switch on the engine, causing a siren to sound in the cab and applying the brake after a short delay. The indication can be cancelled by the operation of a handle. When the distant signal is in the Clear position the ramp is electrified. The lifting of the shoe operates the switch as before, but the current picked up from the electrified ramp causes a bell in the cab of the engine to ring for a short period instead of the siren and without any subsequent brake application.

Eastern Region—London, Tilbury and Southend System

This is operated by magnetic induction. When the distant signal is at Caution a permanent magnet in the 4-ft. way operates the apparatus, sounding a horn and applying the brakes after a short delay. Cancelling or acknowledging by means of a handle provided changes the visual indicator from black to yellow. If the distant signal is at Clear, an electro-magnet is energised which cancels the effect of the permanent magnet, allowing the horn to sound for a short time only and with no subsequent brake application.

British Railways System

The British Railways system also works on the principle of magnetic induction. When a distant signal is at Caution, the permanent magnet operates the receiver on the locomotive, sounding the horn and applying the brake after a short delay. Cancelling or acknowledging the indication by means of a handle provided changes the visual indicator from all black to black and yellow. If the distant signal is at Clear an electro-magnet is energised which cancels the effect of the permanent magnet and causes a bell to ring in the engine cab for a short period.

FORMER GREAT WESTERN RAILWAY SYSTEM

General Description

The primary object of this system is to give audible warning on the engine when the train is approaching a distant signal, or passing a lower distant signal fixed below a "Stop" signal, and the distant signal being in the "On" (proceed with caution) position, also, in the event of this warning being disregarded, to apply the brakes automatically, so as to ensure the train being pulled up before it reaches the home signal.

Another and distinctive audible indication is also given on the engine when the distant signal is "Off" (proceed).

The audible signals given are the sounding of a siren, indicating "be prepared to stop at the appropriate 'Stop' signal", and the ringing of a bell, indicating "proceed normally".

The point at which the audible signals are given is usually about 440 yd. (200 yd. in multiple aspect signalling areas) before the distant signal is reached. Where, however, the distant signal is a lower arm on a "Stop" signal, the audible signals are given just as the "Stop" signal is passed.

The apparatus fixed on the permanent way for operating the audible signals on the engine is a ramp about 40 ft. long, which is fixed between the running rails and is made up of a steel $\perp$ bar mounted on a baulk of timber. The ramp at its highest point is $3\frac{1}{2}$ in. above rail level.

A telegraph wire connects the ramp with a switch in the Signal Box through a contact attached to the distant signal arm.

This switch is attached to the lever controlling the distant signal, so that when the lever is operated to place the distant signal to the "Off" (proceed) position, an electric battery is connected to the ramp, provided the signal has correctly responded to the movement of the lever.

Fig. 87 AUTOMATIC TRAIN CONTROL

Former Great Western Railway System

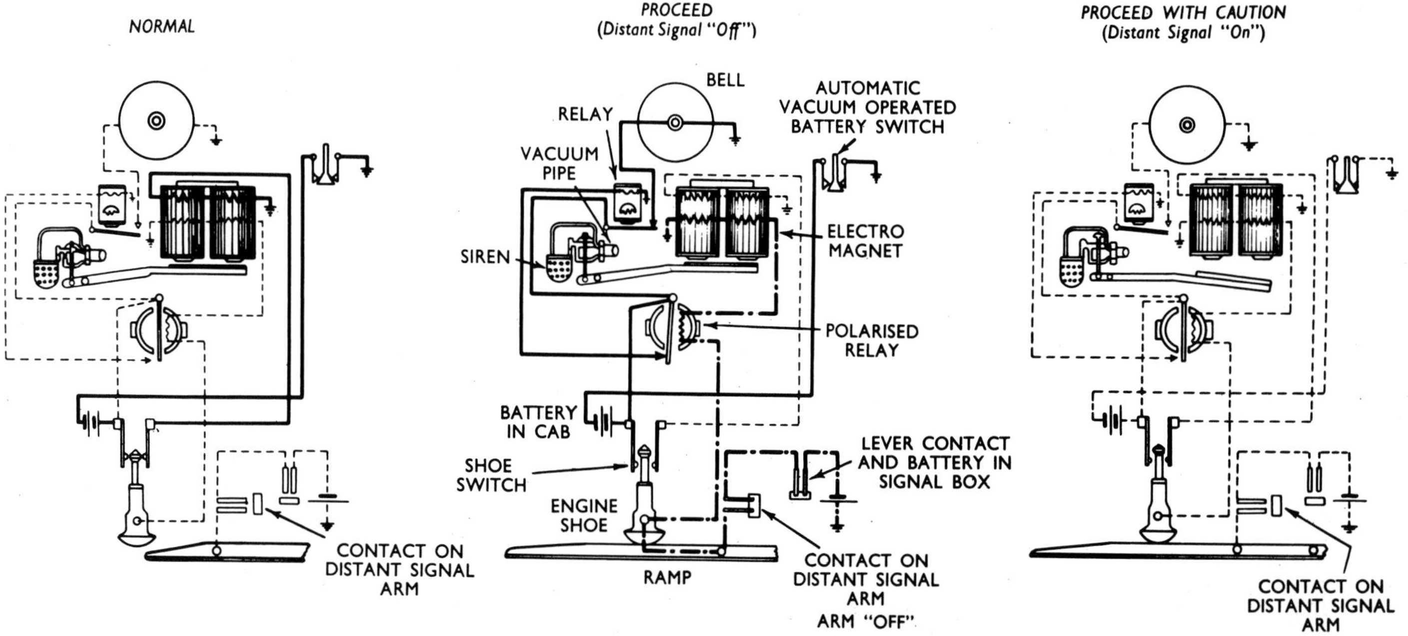

PROCEED WITH CAUTION
(Distant Signal "On")

CONTACT ON DISTANT SIGNAL ARM

AUTOMATIC VACUUM OPERATED BATTERY SWITCH

ELECTRO MAGNET

POLARISED RELAY

LEVER CONTACT AND BATTERY IN SIGNAL BOX

CONTACT ON DISTANT SIGNAL ARM
ARM "OFF"

PROCEED
(Distant Signal "Off")

BELL

RAMP

RELAY

VACUUM PIPE

SIREN

BATTERY IN CAB

ENGINE SHOE

SHOE SWITCH

NORMAL

CONTACT ON DISTANT SIGNAL ARM

Fig. 87

When the lever is replaced to restore the signal to the "On" (proceed with caution) position, the battery is disconnected from the ramp.

The ramp is, therefore, electrified when the distant signal is "Off".

When the distant signal is "On", the ramp is electrically "dead", as is also the case in the event of the battery failing, or the arm not responding correctly to the lever, or the telegraph wire breaking.

The apparatus on the engine comprises a contact shoe with switch, an electrically-controlled combined brake valve and siren, and an electric bell, in the engine cab.

The contact shoe is fixed in the centre line of the engine and projects to within $2\frac{1}{2}$ in. above rail level, in which position it is held by gravity assisted by a powerful spring. It is capable of being raised vertically, and being in line with the ramp it is lifted 1 in. whenever a ramp is passed over. This lift of 1 in. is utilised for effectively opening a switch attached to the contact shoe. The switch is connected with the electrically-controlled brake valve and siren in such a way that whenever it is opened it results, except as hereafter described, in air being admitted through the siren and the brake valve to the train pipe, sounding the siren and applying the automatic brake on the train. This happens when an engine passes over an unelectrified ramp. The Driver, by acknowledging the warning given by the siren, can stop the siren sounding and stop the application of the brakes. This he does by raising a handle provided for the purpose.

When the ramp is electrified by the distant signal being placed in the "Off" (proceed) position, the brake valve is not released by the engine passing over the ramp, but the bell on the engine rings instead. The contact shoe is lifted as before, but the current is picked up from the electrified ramp, the effect of which is to cut out, or render inoperative, the switch attached to the contact shoe; so that although the switch is opened it does not release the valve admitting air through the siren to the train pipe.

When an engine is at a stand and remains thus for more than half an hour, the automatic battery switch operates and cuts the battery off from the cab apparatus, thus economising battery power. This battery switch is operated by the vacuum maintained in the engine reservoir or train pipe. When the vacuum is restored by the Engineman the automatic switch pulls up and closes the battery circuit and energises the cab apparatus.

In the event of a failure to pick up the electric current when a ramp is passed over, the effect on the engine apparatus is the same as though the ramp was not electrified, that is, the valve admitting air through the siren to the train pipe is opened, and the automatic brake is applied on the train, thus ensuring that any failure of the electrical apparatus shall produce the warning indications irrespective of the position of the signals.

EASTERN REGION,
LONDON, TILBURY AND SOUTHEND SYSTEM

Track Equipment

Two magnets are fixed in the centre between the rails, 10-15 yd. apart and approximately 200 yd. on the approach side of a distant signal (or outer signal only when more than one is provided). The first contains a horizontal permanent magnet with its north pole at the trailing end and the second contains an electro-magnet. The electro-magnet is "dead" when the distant signal(s) is at Caution and "alive" with its south pole at the trailing end when the signal(s) has been pulled to Clear. The tops of the magnets are 1 in. above rail level.

In addition to these, permanent magnets are provided in the outlet roads from sheds to test the equipment before going into service.

Engine Equipment

The equipment consists of a magnetic receiver, horn valve, vacuum horn, brake valve, re-setting magneto and indicator.

The receiver is operated magnetically from the track magnets, its internal permanent magnet changing its position and operating an air valve as it passes over the north pole of the permanent magnet or the south pole of the electro-magnet. The re-setting magneto is provided to change it from the position taken up after passing a permanent magnet if the electro-magnet is "dead", as at a Caution signal.

The admission of air through the valve in the receiver operates the horn valve which connects the horn to the vacuum reservoir and causes it to sound and admits air through a restriction to the timing reservoir and lower side of the brake valve.

The upper side of the brake valve is connected to the train pipe so that the valve is normally balanced and kept closed by a spring. The admission of air to the under side upsets this balance and, after 3 seconds, the valve opens to admit air to the train pipe, lowering its vacuum, and the valve assumes a new position of balance such that the fall in vacuum in the train pipe corresponds to the fall in vacuum in the timing reservoir. The fall of vacuum in this reservoir is calculated to reach 5 in. in about 15 seconds.

This action occurs whenever the distant signal is at Caution and

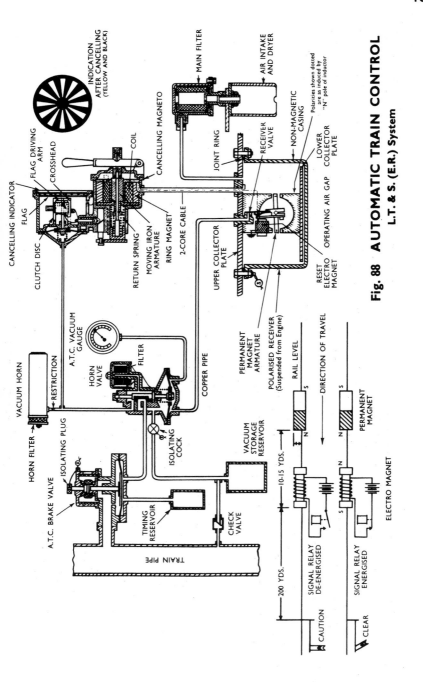

Fig. 88 AUTOMATIC TRAIN CONTROL

L.T. & S. (E.R.) System

Fig. 88

the receiver can be re-set to close the air valve by pulling the handle of the magneto.

If the distant signal is at Clear and the electro-magnet "alive" this would be reached before the brake application started and the act of passing over the electro-magnet would close the air valve in the receiver to silence the horn.

In addition to the audible signals of the horn a visual indicator is provided above the magneto. When a permanent magnet is passed the indicator turns to, or remains, black, but on pulling the handle of the magneto after passing the magnets at a Caution signal the indicator is turned to black and yellow.

Summary of Indications Received

Distant signal at   Indicator black.
Caution   Horn sounds. Brake application starts after 3 seconds. Re-setting changes indicator to black and yellow.
Distant signal at   Indicator black.
Clear   Horn sounds for short time.

BRITISH RAILWAYS SYSTEM

Track Equipment

Two magnets are fixed centrally between the rails, 2 ft. 6 in. apart, generally 200 yd. on the approach side of a distant signal. The first contains a permanent magnet with its south pole uppermost and the second is an electro-magnet. The electro-magnet is "dead" when the distant signal is at Caution and "alive" with its north pole uppermost when the signal has been pulled to Clear. The tops of the magnets are at rail level.

In addition to these, permanent magnets are provided in the outlet roads from the sheds to test the equipment before going into service.

Engine Equipment

The A.T.C. vacuum reservoir is exhausted from the ejector through a non-return valve and isolation cock which is sealed open. An electric switch operated by the vacuum connects the battery to the electrical circuits. The horn is connected to atmosphere through an electrically-operated valve in the Driver's control unit, and the under side of the brake valve and the timing reservoir are similarly connected to the vacuum reservoir. The upper side of the brake valve is connected to the train pipe. The brake valve is balanced by vacuum on both sides, but is kept closed by a spring. If air is

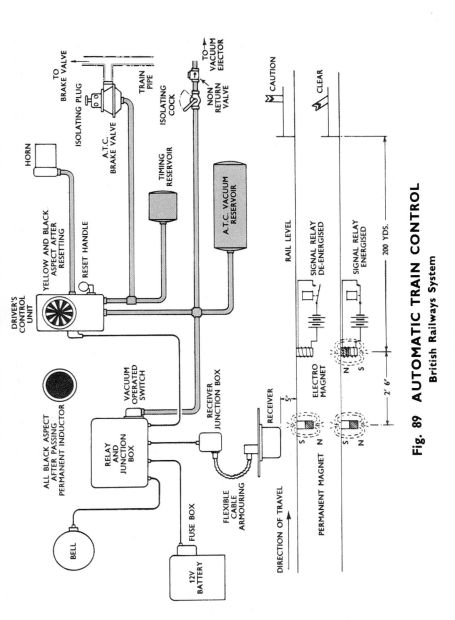

Fig. 89 AUTOMATIC TRAIN CONTROL
British Railways System

admitted to the under side of the valve, the balance is upset and the valve lifts to admit air to the train pipe. The brake valve is sealed open but can be closed by a screwed plug in emergency.

The receiver consists of a permanent magnet carrying contacts which act as a two-way switch, one contact being closed when the receiver has passed over a permanent magnet and the other contact being closed when the receiver has passed over an "alive" electro-magnet.

When running normally the receiver contact closes a circuit to the electrically-operated valve in the Driver's control unit which controls the vacuum and air as described above. When the receiver passes over a permanent magnet the contact opens and after 1 second the solenoid is de-energised and the valve operates to connect the horn to the vacuum reservoir and cause it to blow and also to admit air through a restriction to the timing reservoir and brake valve. This occurs whenever the distant signal is at Caution. The brake valve opens to admit air to the train pipe and assumes a new position of balance such that the drop in vacuum in the train pipe corresponds to the drop in vacuum in the timing reservoir. The size of the restriction and capacity of the timing reservoir are calculated to reduce the vacuum to 5 in. in about 15 seconds. The horn can be silenced and the brake application cancelled by pulling the re-set handle, which re-sets the solenoid and restores the normal contact on the receiver.

If the distant signal had been Clear the receiver would pass from the permanent magnet to the "alive" electro-magnet in less than 1 second (when travelling at more than 2 m.p.h.). In this case the receiver contacts would change over as before on the permanent magnet and change back again on the electro-magnet. As less than 1 second has elapsed the solenoid would not be de-energised to sound the horn or apply the brakes, but the changeover of receiver contacts picks up relays to ring the bell for 2 seconds.

In addition to the audible signals of horn or bell a visual indicator is provided in the Driver's control unit. When the receiver passes over a permanent magnet, current passes to the indicator to turn it to, or keep it at, black. If the distant signal is at Caution and the re-set handle has to be pulled to silence the horn, the indicator changes to black and yellow. The indicator always continues to show the colour set up at one set of magnets until the next set is reached.

Two points should be noted:

    (1) Pulling the re-set handle when not required to silence the horn will apply the brakes.

(2) Pulling the re-set handle will only change the indicator from black to black and yellow after passing the magneto at a Caution signal.

Summary of Indications Received

Distant signal at Caution	Indicator black. Horn sounds after 1 second. Brake application starts after 3 seconds. Re-setting changes indicator to black and yellow.
Distant signal at Clear	Indicator black. Bell rings for 2 seconds.

NOTE.—On both the L.T. & S. Section and British Railways systems the complete magnet and housing which actuate the receiver on the locomotive is referred to as an "inductor".

SECTION 10

THE RULE BOOK

Rules are drawn up for the purpose of ensuring method and order in all movements and operations.

METHOD and ORDER provide SAFETY.

We all know the story of the man who observed two trains approaching one another on the same line, his comment being that it seemed to him a funny way to run a railway!

Railways are the safest means of transport.

The Rule Book has been compiled on the basis of long experience and of common sense. Most of the rules have come into existence on the "case" method, that is, as the result of mishaps and of near-mishaps.

If you find the Rule Book hard to digest you must apply the case method to your study. Visualise a station with which you are familiar, for instance, and imagine a derailed wagon blocking one line. What should be done to ensure protection of the line and how do the rules apply?

It is an axiom that it takes two people's mistakes to create a dangerous situation. Rules aim at preventing misunderstandings. Each man concerned has a definite duty laid down for him to perform.

Any subject may be considered dull when studied in textbooks. Interest is aroused when your reading can be applied to real life and to real situations. Firstly, then, be prepared to visualise.

Secondly, it is helpful to have a proper arrangement in one's mind of the various groups of rules. Sub-divided in this way the Rule Book will appear less formidable and the rules applying to one's particular calling, such as that of Enginemen, can be given special attention.

We can proceed to divide the groups of rules as follows:—

Rules 1 to 16 cover matters of discipline and procedure. Discipline implies a standard of behaviour which is essential to good order in any organisation.

Rules 17 to 33 cover the working of stations.

Rules 34 to 49 describe the various patterns of fixed or permanent signals. Their working and application are, of course, an important part of an Engineman's knowledge.

Rules 50 to 54 lay down the authorised hand signals. Hand signals must be properly given and properly interpreted to avoid misunderstandings.

Rules 55 and 56 are very important safety rules, to ensure that a train standing on a running line is not forgotten.

Rules 57 to 60 cover the use of detonators, which are a form of audible warning signal used where other methods of attracting a Driver's attention are not practicable or need supplementing. A supply of detonators must be on every engine, with two red flags (see Rule 127).

Rules 61 to 76, covering the working of points and signals, must be understood by Enginemen, as they have a joint responsibility in their correct operation. Note Nos. 69 and 70 (*b*), (*c*).

Rules 77 to 80 refer to precautions imposed when signals are under repair, etc., and Rules 81 to 83 cover similar precautions when points and signals are defective. Certain paragraphs are directly applicable to Enginemen.

Rules 84 to 95 ensure the running of trains in safety under the adverse weather conditions of fog and falling snow (see also the special instructions issued in a separate booklet to the staff).

Rules 96 to 98 apply to the movements at stations.

Rules 99 to 107 apply to the working of level crossings.

Rules 108 to 118 cover shunting, where a thorough knowledge of hand signals is essential. Enginemen must observe certain precautions when not accompanied by a Shunter.

Rules 119 to 125 cover the use of lamps. Enginemen are responsible for headlamps and disc-boards and for tail-lamps when light engine.

Rules 126 to 176 cover the normal working of trains. Nos. 126, 127 and 128 are especially directed to Enginemen. Being train-operating rules, the whole of this group concerns Enginemen in their everyday duties.

Rule 177. Reporting of Accidents. This rule introduces the section of the rule book dealing with abnormal occurrences and requires careful study.

Rules 178 to 188. When the abnormal occurs, it is vital to preserve order in the face of emergency. Hence:—

Rules 178 to 181 set out the system of protection.

Rule 182 deals with "Trains divided."

Rules 183 to 185 deal with the systematic removal of an obstruction.

Rules 187 to 188 cover defects on a train.

Rules 189 to 208 deal with the setting up of single-line working. Great care is necessary in this operation and Enginemen should note particularly Nos. 192, 196, 197, 202, 203, 204 and 206.

Rules 209 to 239 cover the precautions to be taken when work is done on the line by the Civil Engineering staff. Enginemen must be familiar with Rule 216, Ballast Train Working, and Rules 217 and 218 in regard to speed restrictions.

Rule 240 should be studied, having in mind the fact that Enginemen, as well as others, are concerned with the conveyance of dangerous traffic.

Certain of the rules are amplified by instructions in the General Appendix, which should be carefully studied.

INDEX

(NOTE: Typical questions and answers are placed at the end of each section—these are not covered in the Index.)

NOTES

NOTES

NOTES

NOTES